Your Life Matters

HOW TO GET OUT OF THE LIFE YOU DON'T WANT AND LIVE THE LIFE YOU DO WANT

Other books by Larry Cockerel:

It's not about cancer, it's about you

It's not about you, it's about those you love

Selling Time! 123 Sales Strategies to Achieve Greater Success Faster

Praise for *Your Life Matters* —

"An excellent, generous book of love from the author's heart and soul of one's life experience. A read for all those who are longing for and wanting their own personal roadmap for change, courage, strength, and confidence as they move forward and feel their value and the much-needed light they will shine on our world."
—Kathy Collins, ASC
Author of *The Mystic Chaplain*

"Larry's book is insightful and inspirational. It will benefit not only those who want to create a new life, but also those who want to improve their already good life."
—Susan L. Farrell
Author on *Self-Empowerment for Women*
www.SusanLFarrell.com

"This book will inspire you, step by step to shake off the negative self talk that is holding you back from being all you can be. Good job, Larry."
—Gary Wilder
Business Owner, Brew Your Own Brew, Tuscon, AZ

"Larry Cockerel has distilled, dissected, and decompressed the message of the ages, that each of our lives matter, into an actionable way to pave a new road for your life regardless of where you are now, regardless of your current condition, circumstance, or situation, because your life matters." —David Norris
Owner, David Norris Leadership, Amarillo, TX area

"Larry gives great insight through personal experience how you can go from hopeless to hopeful. This book shows that by understanding self-worth and purpose, through faith in God and self, you can leave the life you don't want, to the life you dreamed you could have."

—David DeBlock, Business Owner

"I read a good number of books each year and found that an insightful book reveals the author's transformational steps. The author guides the reader on a journey to up-level the reader's life to better serve others. I have known Larry for over 10 years, including sharing those transformational days in Guatemala with The John Maxwell Team, planting seeds of leadership in 20,000 souls yearning to make their life matter. A good leader reveals his vulnerabilities to help others learn and live their own significant life by helping others make their Life Matter! While you, the reader, may have a different set of life experiences than Larry, I firmly believe you will find value in the insights he shares."

—Joe Dutkiewicz, Executive Coach, Founder of Crayon Leadership and Spark Consultancy Group

Your Life Matters

HOW TO GET OUT OF THE LIFE
YOU DON'T WANT AND LIVE
THE LIFE YOU DO WANT

Larry S. Cockerel

HenschelHAUS Publishing, Inc.
Milwaukee, Wisconsin

Published by
HenschelHAUS Publishing, Inc.
www.henschelHAUSbooks.com

ISBN (hardcover): 978159598-611-5
ISBN (paperback): 978159598-672-6
E-ISBN: 978159598-612-2
LCCN: 2018940966

Cover design by Andrew Welyczko

Dedication

I dedicate this book to you, like me, who has screwed up, hit the wall, got stuck in a rut, made many bad choices in life, and have "failure" as your middle name. I wish you great success as your journey continues, and I believe this book is for you!

"Your Life Matters" speaks to those of you who are stuck in a rut, a bad or abusive relationship, a going-nowhere job, bad addiction, prison, or feeling like you're locked up in your own self-made prison and just can't seem to find your way out.

You can get out, stay out, and live the life you truly want! We all have something in common—all 8 billion of us on the planet. We have a story—a sad story, a joyful story—and a message that can change the direction of another's life.
My gift to you is my story.
Let's travel this path together!

Contents

The Year 2020

What a year 2020 was!

I'm writing this on August 15, 2021. We have made it through a whirlwind of a year. Covid 19 and the pandemic hit the world like a raging storm. And it's not over yet. None of us truly know when and if it will ever be "normal" again. The turmoil we are all experiencing is the reason I am updating *Your Life Matters*.

I got it. Yes, Covid 19. I was one of the infected ones—testing positive twice and negative once.

The young lady at the drive-up Covid testing site said to me, "Larry, we're seeing you a little too often. The tests aren't 100 percent and days, it can change. I wouldn't keep testing unless you're really feeling sick. Then you may want to go to the ER." That was my last test—I kept copies of the results for memory's sake.

2020 brought with it so much more than many of us were ready for. The pandemic impacted the entire planet. Everyday, the media reminded us how many cases there were and how many deaths had occurred worldwide and in the United States.

The pandemic brought new words to our vocabulary, or at least provided our conversations with new meanings of familiar words. Here are a few that have stuck with me:

- Self-isolation
- Self-quarantine
- Social distancing
- Social injustice & social justice
- Inclusivity
- Essential workers and businesses
- Mask mandate
- Lock-down
- Pandemic (Sounds scary!)
- CDC Guidelines
- Covid 19 and new variants

The media even started showing images of the virus. How strange is that? As if we might see the virus around the neighborhood and then run for our lives!

There are a few other things that deserve mention. When the schools shut down, we had to learn about Zoom classes and remote learning. Parents had to quickly figure out how to work with teachers in remote class-rooms.

Businesses got to love Zoom and Teams meetings; they could schedule meetings at the drop of a hat, do them remotely, and have workers work from home, saving office rent.

And lest we forget, there were also:

- The Black Lives Matter movement
- The killing of George Floyd and others
- The many heroes: Healthcare work-ers, EMS responders, the care facili-ties, the grocery-store stockers, de-livery drivers, and so many more.

Depression ran rampant. It tripled in US adults amid the Covid 19 stressors:

- Job loss
- Lay-offs and furloughs
- Isolation and loneliness
- Companies shutting down, some forever
- Family members and friends dying.

2020 brought with it so much more. On the positive side, families spent more time together—biking, cooking, finding family activities to do together. People actually started to look at one another and act with compassion. Many companies found that they could change their production practices to make needed supplies for hospitals and help essential workers.

Just one example: Pizza restaurants found that they could heat plastic in the 600+-degree ovens to bend and mold sheets of plastic to produce facemasks and stay in business. Restaurants and stores were able to stay open with curb-side pick-up. And online businesses thrived. Folks found ways to entertain themselves at home. Weddings and other celebrations had to become very creative. Even America's Got Talent adjusted to keep going.

What a year to remember!

I survived the pandemic—so far, anyway. My guess is that if you're reading this, you did as well. My heart goes out to those who lost loved ones. It was so hard for people to remain isolated from friends and family.

Why this Author's Note? This book, Your Life Matters, was written to help people find their way, overcome bad decisions, pick themselves up, keep moving and living, how to make right from wrong. Like so many people during this pandemic, it shows how to pick yourself up and step out into a new life you choose for yourself.

You might still be faced by a setback. Look at your options. Step up and out of the rut you might find yourself in. Stay current with what's happening in the world around you. You can grow though other people's experiences. Remember, you can make a difference, no matter what has happened and where you are in your life today.

Yes, the year 2020 was like a raging storm. Other storms will come.

Together, we can change the world—by first changing our inside world. We can do this!

Your Life Matters!

Larry Cockerel
Cedarburg, Wisconsin
August 15, 2021

Foreword

"For a man to conquer himself is the first and noblest of all victories."
— Plato

So, why am I writing the foreword to Larry Cockerel's brilliant book? I'm a novelist, after all. *Your Life Matters* touched my soul. The author's journey through adversity by sheer determination, and his willingness to share with his readers—not just the bright moments, but the dark ones as well—awakened a kindred spirit in me.

I grew up in the Al Smith housing projects in the Two Bridges neighborhood on Manhattan's Lower East Side. When I was in the fourth grade, my mother was told by the principal of PS-1 that, "Nick was unlikely to ever complete high school, so you must steer him toward a simple and secure vocation." Instead, I became a writer, with a few stops along the way. That's why I wanted to write this foreword.

In the poem *Invictus* by William Ernest Henley, the author proclaims his strength in the face of adversity ("My head is bloody, but unbowed"), and embraces his own responsibility for his future and his life ("I am the master of my fate, I am the captain of my soul"). So too, in *Your Life Matters*, author Larry Cockerel accepts responsibility for his past—and for his future.

Like Henley, Cockerel did not have an easy life. As a teen, he attempted suicide, ran away from home, and lived on the streets. Through his loneliness and despair, he found solace in drugs, which led to theft, which led to prison. Today, Cockerel is a cancer survivor on his way to happiness and fulfillment. *Your Life Matters* is Cockerel's fourth book.

Certainly, neither Cockerel nor Henley were the only authors to speak about the strength to face adversity. Albert Camus said, "In the midst of winter, I found there was, within me, an invincible summer." What all these authors have in common is their willingness to accept bad decisions and adversity, to learn from them, and to take charge of their life moving forward.

To be clear, author Larry Cockerel is not saying you can start over; he is saying you can take charge of how things turn out from this point forward. So too C.S. Lewis: "You can't go back and change the beginning, but you can start where you are and change the ending."

In *Your Life Matters*, Cockerel shows us that "life is a journey, not a destination. The only person you are destined to become is the person you decide to be," according to Ralph Waldo Emerson. And Cockerel does this by using himself as an example. Not just of his achievements, but of his failures as well. He not only gives you a roadmap of our coming journey to success, he shares with you his own failings, thereby, giving you a companion along the way who knows how difficult life can be, a companion who will not judge you, a companion who will assure you that if he was able to make this, the greatest journey of all, so can you.

As you will soon discover, *Your Life Matters*, is divided into seven chapters, each with three steps to follow. To successfully conquer these steps and ultimately transform yourself into the person you want to be, move slowly, both understanding and practicing what Cockerel presents in each chapter.

For example, in Chapter One, Cockerel advises, "As you dive head-first into the book, I hope that you'll stop at a few places, reflect, and ask yourselves some questions: 'Can I relate to this? Who do I know who's experiencing what Larry is sharing?' 'Am I ready to start living the life I really want to live?' 'Am I ready to let go and get out of the life I don't want to live in anymore?'" These questions and others are important to consider before moving on in the book, and your journey.

The order of the chapters is as important as their content, so please do not jump around within the book. Instead, move on only after you have embraced the philosophy and the understanding within each chapter—they build on each other.

Chapter One is "Loving Life." Here, you will be challenged to love yourself, since "it's hard to love others if you haven't found out how to love yourself first." Cockerel also gives you permission "to be okay with who you are, where you came from, and whatever may have happened in your past." In many ways, this is the most exciting chapter because it will get you ready for your future—and it is going to be a good one.

In Chapter Two, Cockerel begins a discussion about believing in yourself by sharing that when he was in his teens and twenties, he knew nothing of self-worth, self-respect, or self-identity. "All I knew was that I wanted to be seen and accepted by others, no matter the act, good or bad."

So how do you begin the process of believing in yourself? Cockerel says "by saying two little words; 'I will!'" And then he presents a list of affirming phrases and suggests that you pick one a day to focus on, and repeat it throughout the day. He also shares his key drivers: belief, courage, and confidence.

He suggests that, in time, as you journey through this chapter of the book, you will develop your own key drivers. While this chapter is inspiring, it is not an easy read. But once you absorb it, you will be well on your way. So, give it the time you deserve to begin to believe in your own potential, accepting that you are valuable, and you are willing to give up on your bad habits. Once you do this, you are ready to have faith in yourself and in others.

The whole idea of faith is covered in Chapter Three, where Cockerel addresses such fundamental questions as, "Why am I here?" "Does my life matter?" and "What is my purpose?"

In Chapter Four, Cockerel turns our attention to letting go "of whatever it is you're holding onto that's holding you back." Now, keep in mind that the author knows how much you might love what is holding you back. He knows, because he has been there. That is one of the reasons he wanted you to conquer the first three chapters before you got here.

That was all basic training. Now, begins the battle, and you know that you are ready for it. Cockerel knew you needed to love yourself, to believe in yourself, to have courage and confidence, so that now you can "become what you believe." It is as simple as saying "if you don't like the road you are on, pave a new one." And while in truth, it is a difficult step to take, the author is still with you, your loyal companion on this new road, encouraging you to keep moving forward. And as he points out in Chapter Five, along this new road keep "thinking right and having a positive focus, not letting anything or anyone slow you down, and know that it is okay to get what you desire in life." "It is never too late to be who you might have been," says George Eliot.

Cockerel begins Chapter Six by telling us "that by the age of seventeen, the average teen in the United States has been told over 150,000 times, 'You can't' 'You won't' 'You're not ready' 'You won't make it' the list goes on." It is no surprise that the author, who was subjected to this as a child and a teen, titled this chapter, "You can do it!" It is easy to understand why Cockerel shares the view (espoused by trainer and mentor John C. Maxwell), that "people never outperform their self-image."

I am not sure I agree with Maxwell or the author here, but then, this is not about me.

And, surely, I can be wrong. But for Cockerel, this is not just an academic exercise. He has lived it, and simply wants to share the way with you.

But how does one go about finding the key to opening the door to one's potential. The author tells us that there are several keys, some of which you will have practiced or mastered by the time you get to this point in the book. Keys like faith, courage, confidence, a positive attitude, to name a few. "Good intentions are good thoughts, but actions and an intentional attitude to move forward are key to your happiness and success."

It is important to fill your mind with the right thoughts using, among other things, "self-talk." Tell yourself every day that, "you can do it," and do not allow any negativity to interfere with your thoughts. "…remove it from your life."

"I have always believed, and I still believe, that whatever good or bad fortune may come our way, we can always give it meaning and transform it into something of value," to quote Hermann Hesse, in *Siddhartha*. We each have the power to change, Cockerel tells us; "…it's simply a choice."

In Chapter Seven, the author asks you to imagine that you are talking to yourself-as-a-teen. I once had occasion to write a letter to the person I was when I was a teen. It was a worthwhile and eye-opening exercise. Here, the author is asking you to do something similar. "So, what would I be saying today to that young teen that might help him find his way." I encourage you to think about that and, if you wish, write a letter to that teen, and perhaps say, "your life matters."

"Transformation is real," the author assures us. How does he know? He is living it now. He is so delighted with the journey, and the results, that he just had to share it. He also is quick to point out that you need other people to help you along this journey. He challenges you to think about who you would like to join you. Also, Cockerel wants you to do an objective assessment of your skills. You will be asked to create a plan to achieve your goals. This will be both challenging and fun. Cockerel says he believes that if he can do it, so can you. "Change your thinking and you can change your life."

In the end, you will find Larry's style engaging and accessible, his advice compelling, and his life heroic and exemplary. "Your Life Matters" is more than just a self-help book; it is a gift with a roadmap, and a companion ready to help you along the way.

For me, way back in the fourth grade, it was a teacher who found me outside the principal's office, listening to the principal telling my mother that I was unlikely to ever complete high school, so she must steer me toward a simple and secure vocation. That teacher spent time with me, telling me to believe in myself, telling me to read everything, and to always eat the icing off the cake (but that's another story). Larry Cockerel is right; your life matters, follow his path, and you will find the life you want. My best wishes go with you.

Nick Chiarkas

author of the award-winning novel, *Weepers* and
Wisconsin State Public Defender Emeritus

Introduction

Hello, my name is Larry. I would like to share with you from my real-life experiences and show that transformation is real. The life lessons I'm sharing in this book have helped me change my thinking and my life; they are realistic and achievable for anyone.

Your Life Matters is a testimonial to the fact that you can get out and stay out, no matter how bad the past has been, how rough you think your life has been, or how miserable the path you're on today. You can change your thinking, attitude, and direction to live the life you really want.

There was a time when I was identified more by a number than by my name. That's what you call doing "hard time." I know, I've been there. You are only known by your number when you're in prison.

Yes, my journey has had many ups and downs, potholes, valleys, screw-ups, bad decisions. It has also had many uphill climbs, peaks, learning, and growth opportunities.

As you join me along this journey, allow me to give you the "short" story first. I believe that you will be able to relate to at least one of these life hurdles, faulty thinking, and bad decisions I've made.

At the end of the day, I truly have no regrets—the decisions and choices I made have helped make me who I am today.

Most of the poor choices started when I was a young teen, in the early 1970s. I attempted suicide, ran away from home, was homeless and lonely. I turned to drugs and theft, led a life of crime and bad relationships. Did I say, screwed up thinking? Oh, yes … I did time in prison, escaped, returned, was released, and found my friend the crack pipe. In addition, I also went through bankruptcy.

Ultimately, though, I am on a path to happiness and fulfillment. Let me share with you how I "got out" and have "stayed out" of the life I didn't want for many years now. At the end of each chapter, I offer three simple steps you can use to take action to get out of the life you *don't* want and start living the life you *do* want.

Know this: when things change and you are down in the valley, you are never alone!

He has sent Me to heal the brokenhearted, to proclaim liberty to the captives, and the opening of the prison to those who are bound.
—Isaiah 61:1

Transformation is real!

1. Loving Life

Love is the greatest gift.

Friends, let me tell you, "I'm loving life"—even with all its bumps, grinds, valleys, disappointments, and scary mountains. I passionately love life!

Before you dig deep into the chapters of this awesome teaching, my mama, Joanne, said, "This is the best book she has ever read since my last one." This one tells the story of how I moved from the gutters of life to building a happy, successful, and rewarding life. And you know mamas don't lie—they tell it as it really is, the real story!

As you dive head-first into the book, I hope that you'll stop at a few places, reflect, and ask yourselves some questions: "Can I

relate to this?" "Who do I know who's experiencing what Larry is sharing?" "Am I really
ready to start living the life I really want to
live?" "Am I ready to let go and get out of the
life I don't want to live in anymore?".

We know that questions lead to answers.
We don't always want to face the answers, or
take action on them. Many times, we may not
know how to take the next step. All that is
okay. You'll be okay, because when you're
truly ready you'll find your way, you'll find
your **why**, your purpose, and your passion.
The purpose of writing this book and sharing
my experiences is to help you along your
way.

At a ripe young age of 59, as I wrap up
this project, I think, "Man, it took me a long
time to find my way, my purpose. Life never
was a race or a destination; it was all about
the journey, the roadblocks, the walls, the
falls, the screw-ups, the bad decisions, and the
good decisions that helped make me who I
am today.

Just like you, all that history helps to make you. It makes up your character, your values, your purpose and passion in life. We humans are kind of like a blended shake. We get all the ingredients stuffed into the blender, shake it up, and blend it up and out pours a great, wonderful creation!

It's a great creation because your life matters, *you matter*, your thoughts, your words, and your plan in life.

There is a reason I wrote this chapter, and wanted to have it be the first chapter you read. The other chapters have many of my life stories and screw-ups and lessons learned. I hope and pray these chapters will help you or someone you know get out of the life they don't want and live the life they do want.

The following chapters might make you think, "WOW! This guy is really a messed-up person."

Not anymore! I let all that go. I got right; I began to believe in myself and my potential. I found faith and began to know I could do it, move into the life I really wanted to live.

My purpose in starting where I'm at today, after 40+ years of being lost and stumbling around, searching for my promised land, is to help you not waste as many years as I did. To help show you that you can make new decisions and choices, and let go of the things that are holding you back, and yes, get out there and live the life you want.

I'm walking proof that it can be done. I've gone from the gray walls of a jail house, through drug abuse, financial disaster, complete lack of self-esteem, and cancer. I've traveled the streets of Corporate America, gone through divorce, and all the other messes—to today, living a happy, debt-free life, serving others, and sharing my life with my best friend and cancer fighter Debbie. We realize our best life is making a difference in other people's lives, helping to encourage others through our cancer battles, maintaining a positive attitude about life, and doing our best to make a difference on purpose every single day!

You may be asking: "Larry, do you love life today?" The answer is yes! Do I have a rough ride every once in a while? Sure. Do I make some blunders along the way? Yes. But the one thing I don't do is kick myself, or put myself down for not-so-good decisions.

I learn something and move on and do my best not to make the same funky decisions again. I believe everyone can love life, pull yourself up by your boot straps, get out there, and discover your skills, strengths and value in the world.

Loving yourself is the most important person to love first. It's hard to love others and life if you haven't found out how to love yourself first. It's okay to be okay with who you are, where you came from, and whatever may have happened in your past.

Once I realized my past didn't define me or make me, I put it behind me. It was just the past. My past life was wrapped up in one big gift of life experiences that would help me along.

You may be facing some tough times, or someone you love and care for is facing some challenges. We all need someone. Everyone has something for someone. My something is my story, my life, and what I've learned that helped me to accept that *my life matters*. I got out of the life I didn't want and today live the life I do want.

The following chapters reveal pieces of the puzzle of my life journey in my early years and even into my late twenties, rolling up to the "Big 30" when I was riding the good Corporate American lifestyle.

I have no regrets and hope that you have no regrets. Life doesn't always make sense. Sometimes things kind of come together. Sometimes they don't.

One of my greatest lessons has been how I think about what is happening in my life, even when I'm the one who puts myself in a not-so-good place. What makes the biggest difference is how I respond or act. My attitude does make a difference, and when I'm the one making the decisions and choices, whether bad or good, my attitude about those choices and myself help keep me moving forward and making things better. A good attitude is always better than a bad attitude, no matter the situation, right?

Chapter 1 is about sharing my present life. We all know the here and now is most important, because today matters. The present always matters more than the past. After all the things life threw my way and all the crap I got myself into, at the end of the day, it's all good. I'm okay.

No matter where you're at, you can be okay, too. It's amazing how with time, we just either hold on to all the old or let it go and live in the present, because today matters.

I hope my life experiences, which will sound really bad as you begin the journey with me in the book, don't have you prejudging me, or thinking "WOW, how can this guy help me?"

My response: My life. My life experiences. What I've learned. What's helped me. At the end of the day, I hope my lessons can help you or someone you know.

We are all here for a greater purpose, and I believe that purpose is to help each other along life's journey, sharing, encouraging and offering a helping hand. This is my helping hand, my way of saying if I can do it, you can do it, and yes, *you can live the life you really want to live, starting right now.*

My recommendation to you now is get started. Move right along to Chapter 2, *Believing in Yourself.* Start turning these pages and enjoy the ride!

Three Simple Steps:

1. Accept yourself just as you are. You're okay!

2. Love yourself with all your heart. Be okay with who you are and what you have to give.

3. Be ready for your best life to come. Your exciting future picture. Get ready!

Walk in love!

2. Believing in Yourself

Your best bet in life is to just believe in yourself.

J ust bet on yourself. Heck, if you won't, can you expect others to? Your best bet is always to bet on yourself; no matter what the outcome is you're shooting for, negative or positive.

There was a time in my life in which I bet I could really screw my life up and that of anyone close to me. What a bad bet, right? Yes, but it was still my bet, and the cards fell accordingly, down and out.

There's a saying among inmates, "If you can't do the time, don't do the crime." I knew many folks who bet that they could do the time and were willing to do whatever crime to cash out on the bet.

That is what I call a negative belief system, not believing the right things about yourself or your life. This is a good bet when you believe you can be more, you will be more, not less. Do the *right* time, not the *hard* time. The right time is leading a good life.

Could this be you?

The crime might not be an illegal one. It may be a crime against your own self-thinking. The crime of self-hurt or self-destruction is one we can put on ourselves— sometimes even intentionally.

So many of us walk around every day, go to work, go home, get into relationships, and have families that are walking jail cells. We are doing hard time with every step we take. This is not much different than prisoners sitting in their cells year after year doing their time.

How do you break out and remove the bars that are surrounding your life?

The first step is believing in yourself, believing you can be more, believing you can make a difference, believing you can step out of the funk you got yourself into.

No matter where you're doing your time, behind cold steel bars or your self-made prison in the free world, you've got to believe you have self-worth.

Many years ago, mostly in my teens and twenties, I knew nothing about self-worth, self-respect, or self-identity. All I knew was that I wanted to be seen and accepted by others, no matter the act, good or bad. That's how stuck and lost I was. I found myself doing time, hard time, with every step in my life, at every turn. The main person I was hurting through my behavior was me.

You've just got to believe in your potential, believe that you can be more and you want to have a good life. Everything that happens starting now will be based on your belief in yourself, your ability to say no, your ability to make good decisions, your ability to avoid peer pressure, and your ability to prevent others from determining your path in life.

Someone once told me, "You have too much potential, too much talent, too much in you, to get stuck in the life you don't want!"

The best I could be was based on how much I believed in myself and believed that I could crawl out of my self-made hole of defeat.

You might be asking, "So, Larry, how did you crawl out?" One step at a time—and one good thought about myself at a time!

So, how do you begin the process of believing in yourself?

You can start by saying just two powerful, little words; "I believe. . . !" They will get you moving in the right direction toward the future. Say out loud, right now: "I believe in my abilities," "I believe in my potential," "I believe I'm worthy," "I believe I can make a difference," and "I believe I'm valuable."

When you state such beliefs every day, such confirmation and permission can help you begin the process of believing in your own words and potential, the power of persuasion.

You are not who people say you are. You are who God says you are and who you think and believe you are and can be.

What you say to yourself is more important than what anyone else can say to you. What you say about yourself determines your attitude, your behavior, and your direction in life. Your words can lift you or bury you— your choice.

The best bet you can make is on your potential. If you bet on you, my guess is that others will bet on you too. Then you will have others pushing, pulling, and encouraging you along every step.

Nothing great has ever been achieved alone. All of us need others saying good things, encouraging us at the same time we encourage ourselves by using the right words, the right phrases, like those listed below.

Check them off every time you state any of these remarkable affirmations. Pick one a day and use it all day as often as you can. Positive reinforcement is okay and good habits begin with the first step. One a day keeps the ..... away!

❑ I'm okay.

❑ I can.

❑ I will.

❑ I'm capable.

❑ I'm trustworthy.

❑ I'm honest.

❑ I'm focused.

❑ I will not do or be what others say.

❑ I'm my own person.

❑ You can count on me.

☐ I care.

☐ I can help.

☐ I believe in myself.

☐ I'm valuable.

☐ I like myself.

☐ I respect myself.

☐ I'm smart.

☐ I can do it.

☐ I will do it.

☐ I'm ready.

☐ I'm willing.

☐ I'm teachable.

☐ I will not be persuaded.

☐ I will not go back.

☐ I'm not a loser.

☐ I'm making something of myself.

☐ I love myself.

The list could go on and on. You can also add to the list and make it your own.

We can find powerful, motivating, and positive words to rule over our life, or we can decide to use words that bring us down—it's a choice. It's just as easy to use positive, encouraging words, as it is to use negative and self-destructive words.

When we learn to believe in ourselves, our potential and abilities, those positive words are just waiting to burst out of our mouths at unbelievable speed! BAM! We can also use these words to encourage others.

For me, there are three key words that really helped make a difference in my life when I was working on getting out of a rut and staying out. These three key words help drive my happiness and success in life and business. At one time in my life, they didn't exist. They were not strength zones of mine. Today, I can proudly say that they are. Belief, courage, and confidence are my key drivers.

Belief. I found that what was most important was that I learned to believe in myself first. I had to believe that I was okay and better than the thoughts that were keeping me down.

Courage. I found that without courage I couldn't believe in myself and reach out for a better life. I had to be able to take risks, move forward, and step out. That takes courage.

Confidence. I found that without confidence in myself, I couldn't take the first step of getting out of the rut. Without confidence, I would have stayed in the "I'm not okay, you're okay" state of thinking. Today, I am in the "I'm okay, you're okay" place, the best state of mind to be in!

You can choose words that move you forward or hold you back.

I know. I'm living proof, with all the crap and negative situations I've put myself through. They stopped my growth, held me back, and caused heartache to myself and others. I know that no matter where you are, what you're facing, hard time, no time, depression, loss—you can still hold your head high. You can determine your thinking and the words that will lift you up and keep you moving forward.

If you haven't done so already, it's your turn to pick the three words that really move you, make you, and help you face life's challenges. No matter how you think about yourself today, you can decide now how to think tomorrow and help you live the life you really want.

Go ahead, I challenge you right now. Stop reading and grab a pen or pencil. Sit back and think about the three words that move you or that you would like to be the words that move you and inspire you. Understand that what you write today may change tomorrow or the next day. No worries, it's okay. We grow and change one day at a time—and change is okay!

The three words I choose to lift and inspire me daily to be my best are:

1. _____

   Why?

2. _____

   Why?

3. _____

   Why?

Once you write your three words, beside or below each one, write the reason why that word moves you, so that you will reinforce your own decision and journey. Keep these words in front of you to create what's called "top of mind awareness." When you're facing something in life or a decision, reflect on these words and reinforce your positive thinking.

A positive attitude is better than a negative one. Positive always wins over!

You might decide to pass over this piece. That's okay. Maybe you're not ready yet. Or you might think to yourself, "I'll come back to it." If so, note the page or do something to remind you, because we all know what happens next—life happens! It keeps on going. I hope you don't wait 40+ years, like I did, to make these positive and healthy decisions.

When you're stuck in a rut, locked up in your self-made prison, you must look deep in your soul to not forgot you are valuable, loved, and have the courage and power to believe in yourself.

Believe you can lift yourself out of the place you don't want to be and have the confidence to march on and run after your dreams.

You may be thinking, "Loved by whom?" Maybe you think you don't have anyone, that you've been left behind or alone. I say you're loved no matter what you've gotten yourself into.

God says, "I'll never leave you." My friend, know that you're loved, no matter what. No matter how bad the crime that got you where you are, no matter how tough life looks to you, *you are loved*.

How do I know this? I remember lying on my bunk, looking out the window between those cold, gray bars, wondering, "Does anyone still love me? Will I find hope and live a good life?"

I was a lost and troubled kid. I had gotten into all kinds of trouble at a very young age and was now doing time. How could anyone love me again? What was love? What was faith? Who was I?

These questions crossed my mind many times for many nights, lying, wondering, with tears in my eyes, what was next in my life? There was no confidence, courage, or believing in myself back then. I was lost, but sooner or later, I would be found. I was blind, not knowing if I would ever see or discover a good, happy life.

At that point in my life, I wasn't much more than an empty shell, going through the motions of a lost and lonely prisoner in so many ways. God wasn't on my mind in those days. Family, who were they? I saw them as "other people," almost like strangers. There was no emotional connection, and I knew they were out there, living their lives, while I was living my twisted, screwed-up life behind bars.

Confidence, what was that?

Courage? I had no clue what that was.

Faith was just a word.

My rut got deeper and deeper in self-pity, and I was lost in my own screwed-up thinking.

At some point, though, I realized everything was my responsibility. It was my life, no one else's. It's my deal of the cards.

Have you ever made up a great excuse or just figured, "I am a victim of circumstances"? Have you ever found yourself making up excuses or not taking responsibility for the rut you're in, or the bad relationship, or whatever screwed-up place you find yourself?

Making excuses and blaming is so easy, isn't it? It doesn't fix anything or get you out of whatever you're in that you know you shouldn't be in. It's not an escape route, it's just what it is, an excuse to not make the right decisions or actions.

I wasn't a "victim of circumstances" at all. All I was, was a person making bad decisions with a funky attitude, not willing to change or even knowing how to change.

I had choices along that journey: stay a victim, a criminal, a prisoner of my actions, or discover that there was hope in a lost soul like me. Hope that I could believe in a better life, a life without chains, a life of value. I had no clue what all that meant, but somewhere in me, I knew this wasn't the life I wanted. I had to believe, believe in me, that deep inside this young, messed-up person, there was something better.

Somewhere along the line, I started to believe that the best bet in life was on me! I think that first seed was planted when the prison chaplain asked *me*—one of more than 1,000 inmates—if I would talk to the mother of an   inmate. The inmate had committed suicide while in solitary confinement, after an attempted escape. James was his name and I knew him. We had been friends.

The chaplain must have believed in me, believed that I was the right person to talk to my friend's mother. Someone believed in me!

From that tiny seed, my confidence started to grow. The shell was breaking open. I felt there was hope for a really messed-up soul like me. I believe now that my thoughts were changing and I began to accept that *my life does matter!*

Then came the courage to do something, to make something, out of my life. The chance came. I was paroled, set free, and was scared out of my mind. I had no plan, no under-standing of how or what to do with my life.

Have you ever felt like you just got set free, the gates of your self-made prison opened up wide for you, and you stepped out, not knowing what was next? It didn't matter if it was pouring rain or you were walking through a snow storm; you just knew you were on your way to someplace different. You were beginning your new life.

You simply knew it was time for a change, and with change, everything gets scary and exciting. That new-found courage set you on your way. One day at a time, one step at a time.

How do you get out and stay out? My three simple steps are:

1. **Believe** in yourself!
2. Find that **confidence** lying deep inside you waiting to burst out.
3. Step forward with your head held high and your new-found **courage**! Don't look back. Keep moving, thinking positive thoughts about yourself, and whatever the vision you have for yourself, don't take your eyes off your target.

Sounds simple, right? It isn't, trust me. It's all worth it at the end of the day.

When you step out, get out, and learn to stay out, your life changes. It might happen slowly, but it changes. Trust me, you'll fall backward, you'll screw up and make more not-so-good decisions again. It is what it is. But you pick yourself up, hold your head high, stand up straight and get moving again.

I love this Bible quote from Philippians 1:28; "Don't be intimidated by your enemies."

Here's what I'm talking about; don't be intimidated by your past, your situation, your addiction—whatever it is you're up against. Don't be intimidated by that enemy. Instead, stand up and face it! Believe in yourself. You can do it.

What I Discovered by Believing in Myself

There is a reason for going from the present— Chapter 1, "Loving Life"—to this chapter— believing in yourself: it all starts inside. Once I started believing in myself, feeling good and okay about me, the transformation began. I began to realize I could be more, do more, and actually live a life of significance.

It started slowly. I had to learn to take responsibility for my life and do good, positive things to prove to myself that I was more than I used to be. I was better than I thought I was.

I had a hunger to do good things for others, too, not just to focus on myself. The more I thought about it, the stronger the hunger became. Good intentions started to fill my life, and a friend recommended that I do some volunteer work.

Someone came up beside me and made a deposit that helped change my direction and my life again! What a wonderful thing. Today, I look for opportunities to come up beside others and make deposits by offering inspiration, ideas, and support.

"Volunteer work?" I thought to myself. I could do that, do something good in the community, help some folks out. I was making good money, was young and single, and there wasn't much holding me back. The big questions were "What?" and "Where?"

I don't remember exactly how it happened, but like stars lining up in the heavens, I began volunteering at the Humane Society. I love animals, and it seemed like they could always use the help.

Next, I volunteered at a runaway shelter for teens. That is where the true change in me began. I had been where they were now. I had walked in their shoes. I believed I could make a difference, maybe just say something or do something that would help one of those teens get his or her life back on track.

My first volunteer job there was driving the bus to take the teens on outings, like bowling or other activities. Working with the staff, I realized that their budget was slim to none, so there were real limits to what they could do for the teens. The businessman in me put on my white hat, and because I had begun to believe I could do just about anything, I stepped up to the plate and volunteered to do more. The plan was to look for ways to get more for the shelter, not just for bowling nights, but gifts at Christmas, birthdays, and other special occasions.

I hit the street and met with clients, quickly realizing they wouldn't just give money to me, but they would to a non-profit. Thus was born "Help of the Rock," a non-profit organization to support other non-profits in Little Rock, Arkansas, and surrounding areas.

Through my newfound ability to believe in myself, I discovered the courage and confidence within to step up to being better and living a better life, a life that mattered.

Fast-forward. From the runaway shelter, I began volunteering at SCAN (Suspected Child Abuse & Neglect) as a hotline operator. There, I listened and helped kids, teens, and parents over the phone. The 1980s saw the beginning of the AIDS epidemic, and I got certified to teach AIDS Epidemic Awareness. I was following a purpose-driven mission, and belief in myself grew every day.

My message here is that you must find activities or things you can do in your life that interest you, that become a hunger, that help develop your self-worth. You need to let that inner faith blossom, along with the courage to step out and be more and do more and live a better, more fulfilling life.

Helping others doesn't need to take a lot of money. Sure, setting up a non-profit organization took a few hundred dollars. What was more valuable was the time invested. Time is our most precious commodity. By giving of my time, my self-esteem grew, and I was on my way to a better life.

Today, Debbie and I volunteer at the Milwaukee Rescue Mission, the Salvation Army, and cancer-oriented organizations.

There is always a group or organization that can use your help, your passion, your time. Build on the power of believing in yourself.

On my office walls are awards to remind me of the good deeds accomplished while I was finding my way. Here are just a few:

- Governor's Volunteer Excellence Award, State of Arkansas, signed by Bill Clinton (the Clinton days in Arkansas)

- Certificate of Merit Award from Arkansas in support of SCAN

- Certificate of Merit and Training, University of Arkansas for AIDS Awareness Training.

There are many more acknowledgments on my "wall of fame." They inspire me to seek out opportunities to make a difference on purpose.

Three Simple Steps:

1. The first step is **believing** in your potential, your abilities, and your place in the world.

2. The second step is **accepting** the fact that you are valuable, you are im-portant and unique, and you can add value to others!

3. The third step is stepping out of the old you, **letting go**, and loving and believing in the new you. Step out and up. You can do it.

Believe you can,
and you can get out of the life
you don't want, stay out,
and live the life you do want.
Your life matters!

3. Finding Faith

Faith was the hardest thing to find.

Yes, faith was the hardest thing for me to find. But I found it. For me, this is the most important chapter in the book and in the story of my life—finding faith!

Looking back, I now understand why. If I only had that magical crystal ball, right? Well, I didn't, just like you don't and won't. It doesn't exist. What a big surprise, hey?

At first, I couldn't find faith, because I wasn't looking for it—that was my first problem. I thought faith was something you could only find in a church. Back in my early days, the only time I went to church was when my folks took us there on Sunday mornings. It was what you're supposed to do down south in the Bible Belt!

As I grew up and got out from under my parents'—or should I say my step-dad's—roof, I drifted away from church.

Have you found faith?

Once upon a time, I was lost, and then was found, was blind, but now I can see. I had to discover faith in myself first, before I could find it in anything or anyone else.

This step wasn't an easy one and took over 40 years of roaming around in the wilderness to start figuring it all out. I hope a few pages and a little reading time won't take you that long!

To get out and stay out, I had to figure out that faith is in. In what? In me and you and every person who crosses our paths every day. Faith was one of those things I have thought about for 40 of my 59 years.

Sure, I knew what it was and what it was supposed to mean. I didn't fall off the truck yesterday, you know. Back in my "inmate" days, the chaplain told us that faith is believing in something or someone you couldn't see. That faith was believing in something bigger and more powerful than me or you, or any living soul wondering about the planet.

I wish I would have heard that message and understood the power in it a lot sooner. I bet my life would have taken a different path.

For by grace you have been saved through faith and that not of yourselves; it is the gift of God, not of works, lest anyone boast.
Ephesians 2: 8, 9

What a powerful message regarding faith, "as a gift of God." I didn't understand God's gifts in my early years and in so doing, I missed out. Yes, I missed out on the gift of change and direction in my life. I also understand and accept that the direction I took helped make me who I am today. No regrets!

The word "pardon" in prison terms means being set free, let go, forgiven by the state. With regard to faith, being pardoned means being forgiven for your sins. Set free. Released from your past. You are being pardoned for your sins by God. My friend, I found that I was pardoned by my faith and set free to live the life I wanted. I began to believe my life mattered, and I believe *your life matters too*!

I had to figure this all out on my own, whether behind bars or in the free world, or a prisoner to different addictions, bad habits, and not understanding myself. Perhaps you have experienced something like I have in some form or another: a bad relationship you should have gotten out of years ago, an addiction of some kind, a life of crime, or just living a very lonely, sad life.

Maybe, on the other side of the coin, you're a very wealthy, successful, and unhappy billionaire. Maybe you have everything that life can offer—fancy cars, big mansions, more money than you can blow in a lifetime, or a relationship based on all you can get out of each other.

I don't know where you are in life's confusing and challenging journey. I just know where I've been and where I don't want to go ever again. To get out and stay out, you must have faith in yourself, in your God, in those who love you, in others, and faith in the process of personal growth and development.

Think carefully about the next question. Have you ever thought you were the wrong person on trial? Sure you have. I know I have and let me tell you, go sit in a jail house for a day or so, and you'll discover that everyone behind bars was the wrong person on trial.

Today I know where I'm at in life is where I'm supposed to be, even though it doesn't make sense or doesn't feel right or look right at times.

There were times I set myself up for failure, just doing things I knew were not right or were not taking me in the right direction. Today, I don't kick myself for those decisions. I can see clearly now why I made them. They helped make me who I am today, as crazy as they now seem.

Next, I'm going to share a very powerful lesson with you. Are you ready? Be sure to dog-ear this page or mark it in the front of the book—however it is you like to keep up with these defining messages. The next statement is a big one—what some might call a "tipping point."

The inside always affects the outside.

Learning this life lesson took many years and many ups and downs, and certainly more downs than ups. What was on the inside was shaping my external experience. What was on the inside were my thoughts about me, my attitude, my self-esteem, my faith in myself, as well as my faith in God. The inside me affected the outside me—my behavior, attitude, friendliness to others, basically everything on the outside reflected the inside thinking.

I realized I had to change my thinking if I was ever going to get out and stay out of whatever crap I was standing in!

Sounds pretty simple, right?

What sounds simple at times really isn't. It takes faith first, and acknowledging what a mess you're in. Ask yourself; "Do I have the faith in myself to get out and stay out of the mess I've gotten myself into?"

Faith is in, really in! It's okay. It's cool to have faith. Faith in you, your God, the weather—whatever it is you need to have faith in to help you get to where you want to go in life.

Have you ever just gotten stuck in a situation that makes you think, "How in the world did I get into this mess?" Of course you have. You're human. Maybe it's a bad relationship, a dead-end job, a financial hole.

Or maybe you think people are always talking about you or looking at you strangely.

Maybe you're just stuck in determining what your purpose in life is, or if you should believe in God. Maybe you're unemployed and don't know what to do. Maybe you're simply feeling screwed up and lost.

I've got the answer, the secret key to opening the door of opportunity and helping you get unstuck. Here we go again! This is a good one, and it works!

No matter what happens to you, there is a purpose, a lesson, a teaching to help you fulfill your destiny.

It's an acceptance thing: accepting that what happens to you is driven by a purpose and a lesson to lift you.

Once you have faith and accept that all that happens and or comes your way has a purpose, you have a key to unlock the door and discover your potential. It may not look like it, smell like it, but it is what it is.

Another powerful lesson that has helped me in my faith is knowing that God doesn't waste any experience. He doesn't waste what you've been through. He'll use you to help others who are dealing with the same situation.

I've got a lot of stories of how I hit the wall, dug myself into a deep hole, found myself behind bars, on the streets, strung out and broke, but you don't want to read about all that stuff, or do you?

My mentor and friend, John C. Maxwell, bestselling author and speaker on leadership, says, "If you want to impress people, talk about your successes; if you want to help people, talk about your failures."

I did not write this book to impress you. I'm writing to help you get out of whatever undesirable situation you're in and then stay out.

Let me tell you, I've been in so much bad stuff over the years, as you've read so far. I'm personally responsible for my actions. I can't blame anyone—the law, the weather, the economy, or anything else—just me.

And I found that taking responsibility is the first step of a 12-step program, like Alcoholics Anonymous.

Without faith, I'm not sure where I would be today. Most likely not writing and trying to help make your path through life better.

Wouldn't it be great to find out where all the potholes are before you set out on your travels so you know where not to go?

Life is funny. It doesn't work that way. All of life's ups and downs are worth it. They are all part of the big picture of learning, growing, and changing along life's roller-coaster ride.

John C. Maxwell, says, "Everything uphill is worthwhile." I believe it's better to have "uphill thinking" than "downhill thinking."

I've done enough of the latter in my life. Little faith is needed in that kind of thinking.

I write because I want to add value, to help others discover their magic, get unstuck, and get out of whatever rut they may be in. I want to help others get out and stay out. The first step in the process is faith.

Yes, faith. It's in you, all around you, above you, below you, in others and most importantly, God has faith in you. You can be the best you can be!

As I write about "finding faith," I'm not just talking about spiritual faith, or just faith in a religion. I'm also talking about faith in yourself. I call this "Self-Faith." This is the faith you have in yourself and your abilities, the faith you have that you can change and that you can move forward. This self-faith is critical to your happiness, personal development, your ability to handle change, and to build a better future life. You've got to have faith in yourself before you can have faith in anything else. Faith begins within.

In 2008, I was diagnosed with head and neck cancer. The doctor told me I needed surgery fast, as it was already Stage IV cancer. He also told me I needed chemotherapy, radiation, and a feeding tube during the treatments, followed by weeks of recovery afterwards.

Faith? I needed to have faith in my cancer-fighting team, in myself, and in God, to help me fight the big C. It was "self-faith" in action.

Here are three questions for you regarding your life, your destiny, and your legacy. These three questions alone are worth your investment in this book.

These three questions are about self-faith, because you need to have faith in yourself to work through them and with them. If you have spiritual faith in God, I believe He will help you with your answers and provide clarity if you'll allow Him to.

The Three Questions About Your Life:

1. Why am I here? (This is a question regarding your purpose.)

2. Does my life matter? (This is a question regarding your significance.)

3. What is my purpose? (This is a question regarding intention.)

Let me tell you, finding the answers to these questions isn't easy. I'm still working through them myself. I've been working on them for a while and have just about completed the first one about purpose. This is the reason I write: I hope to help others and add value.

The second question—does my life matter? I hope so, as I write and work with groups, I believe I'm adding value and becoming more significant in my purpose.

Now to the third question, purpose and intention. This is the one that truly is a daily activity of being intentional about my purpose, significance, and life plan. You've got to have a plan!

I hope you have the faith to step up to answer these questions and allow the answers to be a part of your daily life. Self-Faith is the first step. It's more than okay to have faith in you, God, others, the system, and in the power of defining the three questions regarding life.

Give them a shot. I have, and by discovering my answers, I'm finding my way. It's important to find your way through life, right? Either I'm finding my way, or I'm lost, looking for the right path.

There was a time in my life that I had zero self-worth, zero self-esteem, zero faith, zero confidence, and zero courage to do anything about it, other than just reinforcing my negative self-image. Sometimes I'm amazed that I'm still walking this planet alive and a free man.

From being a runaway teen, to getting into a life of petty theft, to becoming addicted to all sorts of drugs, to robbery, to causing deadly harm to another person—I was screwed up. It was what it was. I didn't know how to get out of the turmoil and bad situations.

It took many years of hitting my head against the wall, setting myself up for failure, and doing all the wrong things to get the wrong results. I have no desire whatsoever to walk in those shoes ever again.

Faith—what is it worth? It's worth everything. Faith and love are the two main ingredients to creating a life the way you want, and getting out of whatever it is you're in and staying out.

Finding faith and loving yourself help you have confidence and courage in yourself, because *your life truly matters!*

Years passed before I realized I had potential to be more, do more, and just maybe, live a life of significance, a life of helping others, putting others first. Moving in this direction took faith in me. Actually, it had always been there. It took other people to stand beside me, encourage me, speak words of faith in me, and words of love.

It's always been my choice to accept or reject what others said about me. So often I heard "You can't …" "You're a bum…" "You're a loser …" "You'll never amount to anything…" Those words didn't make me; they were just words and I had the choice to accept or delete them. Through faith in myself, I began to hit the delete button, to dump the negative memories in the trash can, and learn to move forward with faith in myself, God, and others.

Other people came along and said things like, "You can do it …" "You're a good guy…" "You're a special person…" "I'm proud of you…" "I love you." These are words we all need to hear—and to tell others as well. We can each plant the seeds of hope and encouragement.

You can do it, too. You can be more, have more, give more, dream more, change more, lead more, and be happier, more successful, and really make a difference in the world. It's all achievable. Have faith, then love yourself, believe in yourself, develop your confidence, and have the courage to step up and out of the rut that is holding you back. Have a little faith!

To wrap up this chapter, I offer you this quote. It's really about deep faith.

Let what is coming to you just come to you. Don't hurry time, destiny, and life.
– Author Unknown

Three Simple Steps:

1. The first step is in having faith in yourself that you can live the life you desire, the life you really want.

2. The second step is being okay with your spiritual faith. Hold it, live it, and be proud of your faith. Faith is in!

3. The third step is in having faith in others, and accepting the fact that you can't do it all alone. Nothing great has been achieved alone—and you're great. Faith is about believing in what you can't see, and that is your future's exciting picture.

Faith. What's it good for? Absolutely everything!

4. Letting Go

Letting go is a step in the right direction.

Yes, you read that right. Letting go of whatever it is you're holding onto that's holding you back is a great place to start.

Early on, I held onto all the crap. I held onto the negative thinking about myself, my disposition, my place in life, my self-pity. I let all that crap pull me down and move me in the direction of self-destruction.

Once upon a time, right?

The worse I got, the better I thought I felt, the more wrong the better, the more rebellion and fighting my internal battles drove me right down in a hole. Poor me, right? Wrong!

You may be able to relate with what I'm talking about. We've all got a bad-luck story: "not my fault," "my bad environment," "my lack of family," "my sad background." A good gardener pulls the weeds so the flowers can grow. I seemed to want to plant the weeds, if you know what I mean.

I went from bad to really bad and then to an all-time low. Letting go wasn't part of the plan. That's why I ended up where I did. It was my fault, my stuff, but I didn't care. I was on the path to self-destruction.

You're probably thinking, "WOW! Is this supposed to be a motivational, uplifting, and inspirational message about getting out and staying out, or just Larry's bad-luck story?"

It's both. Why? If all I shared was my successes, it would all be about me. That would be pretty boring and only fill a few pages in the book.

Over the years as a trainer and speaker, I've found that transformation is about my failures, losses, and downfalls. When I share how I climbed out of the hole and shook off all that dirt, cleaned myself up, polished my attitude, and started moving forward, that's what brings transformation. I've got to share it all—what got me there and what got me out.

Most of my mentors share what they learned from their experiences and life lessons; they didn't talk all about themselves and what they achieved, or spout off a bunch of ego crap. They openly and honestly tell what didn't work, how they screwed up, and offer all those bad decisions, to help others hopefully not make the same mistakes.

I had to let go—let go of living in the past and begin looking toward the future. I had to focus on my dreams and what would be my purpose in life. Yes, me—a two-time loser, former drug addict, a big-time loser in my own definition of a loser!

The worst thing in life is to look back and think of all the things I could have done, should have done, and didn't.

What I did learn along my journey was that you can be in prison—brick-and-mortar or self-made—but you can't imprison a dream!

You may be asking, "What's a two-time loser?" That is what inmates are called when they come back for a second time. Bad stuff, right?

You may be thinking, "Larry, what could you have done to get locked up?" Well, there were a number of things. But today, those past evil actions aren't what's important. Nuff said.

I had to look deep in my soul, and work through a bunch of stuff trying to find a better me. Hopefully, I would find someone who could be somebody someday. I remember nights where I would lie on my bunk and look out the bars with tears in my eyes wondering if being in prison was going to be my life story?

Was I at the end of the line? Had I made up my mind that my life was to be like this forever? Was my life just going to be this, nothing, almost nonexistent?

I began to accept the thought that maybe this was my destiny; I would forever be a person with no purpose, nothing, just leading a lonely life of crime, drugs, and self-pity. Was this a weird form of mental rehabilitation or was I becoming institutionalized?

I hoped not. Being "institutionalized" means you're coming back. Getting out and staying out wasn't the plan, if or when you got released. For some, getting released was just a short-term vacation. Maybe it was time to go commit another crime to come back tougher with a longer sentence, and the ego-driven, screwed-up thinking of "I'm back" and "I'm bad." "Look at me now."

The old saying in prison was, "If or when I come back, it'll be for a tougher crime and longer sentence." Baby, it's time for graduation to the Big House. Stepping up to the big time.

Many are not able to let it go. They come back, rather than getting out and staying out. When a person does time and gets out, it's a choice to stay out or return. That's why the stats show that more than half of those incarcerated who get released come back with worse crimes and longer sentences.

I was one of these statistics. I put myself right in that place. I had never met my biological father, but somewhere along the line, I learned he had done time for bank robbery. I wondered if I were like the dad I never met; I have his DNA. Maybe I'm destined to a life of crime, too.

For many, that is the way of prison life and how to build a feeling of importance and success. Some of those released would come back six to ten months afterwards, walking down the halls, talking with people they knew, getting recognition from fellow prisoners, who'd say, "I knew you were coming back." A return brought laughter and an attitude of success in the life of a convict—in prison terms. Sad stuff, right?

* * * * *

Your prison may not have physical bars. You could be in a bad relationship. You could be struggling with addiction. You might be in a job you hate, one that has no future. Or you might even be held prisoner by your lack of self-worth and self-esteem. Not all prisons have bars and guards and chow lines and hoe squads and cotton fields.

Whatever your prison looks like, know that you can *get out and stay out*. You've just got to find your way, find a purpose to keep you moving toward the light at the end of the tunnel. Taking one step at a time in the direction of your dreams or your vision for a better life.

Early on, I didn't know what my purpose was, or if I even was ready to be released. In life, there are two choices in most situations; fight or flight.

My first time down, I chose flight, not fight. There was nothing to fight. I was where I was supposed to be in life, there or death I guessed. I've heard it said many times: "Larry would have either ended up killing himself or someone else, or in jail." Neither a good choice, but jail was the better of the two.

Looking back, I was already in jail—my own self-made jail cell, before I even entered the real, cold, gray prison walls and barbed wire fences.

Have you ever felt like you have built your own prison cell, locked it up, and thrown the key away? More times than I can count, I heard my fellow prisoners say, "Hell, it's okay. I get three meals a day, a bed, don't pay taxes, and have less hassles."

This way of thinking is really all screwed up to me, but for some, it's their reality.

Getting out and staying out wasn't on their minds and might not ever be.

Actually, it is very scary to think of the crimes some people commit just to return to prison for a longer stay and a tougher sentence.

I know there was a time along my crime-filled journey that I wasn't ready for the "free world." The "free world" wasn't in my sight. I couldn't even comprehend what to do without the structure of prison life. What would my life on the outside look like?

That was as scary as hell—maybe it was better to be locked up and safe, than set free and being lost.

If you don't know who you are, you just might be better off in your own prison, because that's where you are anyway. I know all about get out, stay out, because I got out. But I didn't stay out.

Hell, it was worse than that. I was 45 days from my release date and ran. You got it. "Flight" in all its glory. Only 45 days to freedom, the free world, and I chose to escape!

How screwed up and messed up is that?

The rule is getting out and staying out, not get out and don't leave, or get out and hurry back, or get out and come back laughing, walking and talking tough.

For many, that's the life prisoners think of as successful and big-time, coming back time after time, just waiting for their personalized bullet or life sentence.

Looking back, I came up with a couple of good titles for this book: *45 Days to Freedom*, *8 Miles to Freedom*, *Lost and Not Found* … the list could go on and on.

Prison is actually where I learned to appreciate reading. I also learned to look up to others with longer sentences, tougher crimes, better job duties, and trustee jobs. I think I've always had a little bit of "leader" in me. I landed many good job duties, achieved trustee status, got to hang at the back of the hoe squad line and talk with the "Boss Man" on his horse. My job was to clean up the rows by removing weeds that were missed, following up behind the rest of the convicts.

I was slowly moving out and didn't even know it. I had leadership qualities, but couldn't see them, because of where I wanted to see myself and that was as a prisoner—not a person or a leader.

This book might have been a gift to you from someone who cares about you, someone who wants to help you get out and stay out of your rut, who wants to help you better understand yourself and move in a positive direction with your life.

I believe you are a leader, a person of value with great ideas and self-worth, a person who can make a difference in the world. You just haven't given yourself a chance yet.

This is what I know now, and it's a very powerful and valuable lesson. These three words are worth the small fee you paid for this book. *Your life matters!*

Become what you believe!

Doing so is pretty simple and very difficult at the same time, but I found that I did become what I believed, good or bad, it was what it was!

The second life lesson I learned along with that one was

When your thoughts are better, your life will be better.

Change your thinking and change your life. That seed of truth began to grow and my thoughts began to change a little at a time. Maybe there really was something good and valuable deep inside me that would grow. Maybe I could catch it and run with it one day!

What about you?

* * * * *

Now back to some of that prison stuff, just in case you've never been to a prison. Let me define a few terms for better understanding. I hope that these definitions will help you grasp my story a little better. Street terminology isn't always easy to comprehend if you're not familiar with it.

- **Hoe Squad**: This is a group of inmates who work as a team in the field with a hoe, digging ditches, cleaning out the weeds in bean fields, cotton fields, corn fields, or whatever was growing at the time. The Hoe Squad was comprised of anywhere from 8 to 20 inmates.

- **Boss Man**: This is the guy (guard) on the horse with a gun, yelling at you, talking about you, and watching over you as you worked. Think of a "chain gang" from the movies. Having prisoners do the work is big in the South because of the farming.

- **Free World**: Term used by convicts (inmates) to designate the outside world. As we know, so many people are not free, because of self-made prisons in which they spend their entire lives. In some cases, this may be worse than prison itself.

- **Trustee:** This is a position the select few are able to earn. They can work without guards in certain positions throughout the prison grounds and different departments. Some buy this position and many earn it.

I got the trustee role inside first, watching over the main floors and barrack gates, letting inmates in and out of the barracks. Then I got moved out to the rice fields, where my first step to freedom became the end. Outside in the fields, away from the main housing unit, was where the great escape went down. What a mistake, right? Only 45 days to freedom!

It was me running nowhere, really just running back. I didn't know it then, but really deep within, I wasn't ready for the free world. Had I truly gotten "free," looking back, it would have been terrible and might have been the end of me.

Getting out and staying out wasn't in my plans at that time. Instead, "The Hole," also known as "solitary confinement, " was home for 30 days after they caught up with me.

John, the other inmate who made the great escape with me, and I ran through the rice fields where we were stationed, with no real idea of our destination. We followed a river, then found a road and followed that. We were tired, hungry, and scared. We made it about 8 or 10 miles west of the prison grounds.

There was a school we found to hide in that night. By morning, they had found us. Twenty-four hours of freedom. We were captured!

* * * * *

The Lesson: Let go! Let go of all the funky thinking and ego-driven, negative attitude. Let go of the thoughts that you are where you are and are unable to change that. Stop the "stinkin' thinkin'."

If you're in prison and sentenced to a term where you know one day you're going to be set free and your sentence is going to come to an end, it's all about letting go.

No matter what your prison looks like, you can find freedom, no matter where you are.

Prison bars or no prison bars, freedom is a choice, a state of mind, an attitude, and way of life.

Letting go! Know you can grow and accept change. Let go of the negative thinking. Take responsibility. Look for the good within you. Become the best you can be right where you are.

Let go of the peer pressure, the wanting to look tough and bad. Let it go. Let go of the feelings of self-defeat, of being undervalued and underappreciated. Changing your life means changing how you see yourself, how you think about your value, how you appreciate and love yourself. Those things are what matter.

I know this because I've lived in the "I'm Not Okay, You're Okay" life position. I've lived in the screwed-up thinking of, "What do I have to offer anyone or the world?"

Let it go. You are a person of value, a person with ideas, no matter if you have a life sentence, or a self-created prison in your own home, relationship, job, or life.

This is what I know. Each of us can be more than we are today. We can learn new skills. We can find love and a career that's not filled with crime or failure. We can climb out of the deepest hole we can dig for ourselves.

I did. No real education, no direction, no plan, no understanding of my purpose or future. I had to let it go—let go of all the bad attitudes, screwed-up thinking, self-pity, and ego.

I had to find humility. I needed to be grateful that I was alive and to know that someone was out there for me.

Read the following statement really slowly. Believe you can do it.

If you don't like the road you're on, pave another one.

The message really says, "If you don't like where your life is going, change it!" Your life matters, so make some new decisions, stop hurting yourself, pick yourself up, and get moving forward.

We all have the power to make the decisions that either break us or make us. All it takes is making a decision. You can take that to the bank!

You can be more than you are today. You can tear down your prison walls. You can remove the bars that hold you back. You can find hope and purpose. You can make a difference in the world and be a person of value, *if you choose*.

And most important, let it go! Let whatever it is holding you back go, no matter what it is. Let it go!

The story of Mr. Johnson: Once upon a time, Mr. Johnson worked for a respected company. He worked from 8 a.m. to 5 p.m., got two weeks' vacation and earned a discount on his health insurance. He sat in a cubicle all day long. He was told when he could eat, how he would dress, and what he would work on and when.

But Mr. Johnson dreamed of freedom. He dreamed of being fulfilled by his work and he dreamed of being in control of his time, money, and skills. Then one day, he was.

How? Well, as the story goes, Mr. Johnson let go and reached for his freedom, his dreams, and began living the life he wanted to live! His choice was to let go of an unhappy and less desirable life to reach for a new exciting life. You can too!

Life can be this way—a free life of following your dreams, passions, and true desires. It's up for the taking for anyone, at any time.

Self-made imprisonment can be like a hamster in a cage, running on a wheel, never really getting anywhere. Don't live your life like a hamster, running on a wheel getting nowhere! You are a masterpiece from the almighty God. You can be the best you can be and live the life you really want!

If I can, you can! I give you permission right now to live the life you want to live.

Three Simple Steps:

1. The first step to freedom is letting go of what's holding you back.

2. The second step is to begin stepping forward in faith, courage, confidence, and believe in yourself that you'll be okay!

3. The third step is to simply keep moving forward with a positive attitude and a clear understanding of where you want to go and how you're going to get there.
   At the end of the day any movement forward and out of the life you don't want to the life you want is a success step.

A step a day is the way,
so keep stepping
along your way!

5. Getting Right

Life is full of choices.
The choices you make —
make you!

Slow down and read those words again carefully. It's about getting right upstairs!

I'm not talking about getting your upstairs right, like cleaning your room, or closets, not your home upstairs, but your mind, your attitude. That can determine just about everything you do from this point on in which you choose to change.

It doesn't matter where you are in life, what path you're on, what prison cell you're sitting in, man-made or self-made. Your attitude will direct your behavior and your habits.

"All significant battles are waged within the self."

—Psychologist Sheldon Kapp

We can definitely win those battles when we change our approach.

Early on, my attitude about myself sucked. I was locked into the life position of "I'm Not Okay, You're Okay" crap. Nothing good comes from this state of mind or attitude but self-destruction.

The path of self-destruction is an easy path—not much responsibility is needed, laziness is accepted, hurting others around you is normal, and the choices made are typically terrible ones. I know through experience, trust me.

Get right or get out! That might be something a boss, a spouse, a friend would say. Get right or get out of the relationship, the job you're stuck in, the life position you're so unhappy to accept.

Allow me to share the four life positions you can find yourself in, based on your choices. These were originally introduced by Thomas Anthony Harris, in his book, *I'm OK, You're OK*.

1. I'm Okay, You're Okay
2. I'm Okay, You're Not Okay
3. I'm Not Okay, You're Okay
4. I'm Not Okay, You're Not Okay.

If you're not at number one, which is the best place to be, then make the choice to get out of one of the other three and move to life position number one.

Number four is the worst place you can be. This is a self-destructive, negative attitude that can even lead to suicidal behavior and can or will hurt you and all those in your life.

Hear me on this. I was there in the early 1970s. I wanted to kill myself and attempted suicide. Two handfuls of sleeping pills put me in a coma for three days. I found myself on the floor in a hospital psychiatric ward. I was only 13 or 14 at the time. Not the place to be at any age.

For most of my life, I was stuck in life position number three, with very low self-esteem, image, and low motivation to change. It was easier to go with the flow. I sought attention in just about any way I could find it—crime, drugs, and more—thus putting myself in the environment that reinforced my thinking and attitude.

"Getting right" takes effort, takes determination, takes love for oneself, and takes what I call "self-love." What I mean by "getting right" is fixing your attitude about yourself. Improving your ability to think in a more positive way. To accept the fact that no matter what, you are a valuable human being. Your life matters!

When you look at the world around you in a more positive way, you can work with others and not always be the one who pulls everyone down. No one likes to hang with a trouble-maker but a trouble-maker. No one likes to hang with a negative-thinking and negative-talking person but one of the same.

If you're looking to get out of a rut, a hole you've dug deep, your prison cell, your unhappy life—then you've got to *get right*. It's pretty freaking simple—no screwing around. Your attitude is simply a choice.

I asked a few friends what the phrase *"Getting Right"* meant to them. Jeffrey said, "Getting it right the first time." My friend Sue said it meant, "Stop screwing up and grow up!" WOW! I like that one. She must have known me when I was a screwed-up youth!

If I were to ask you what "Getting Right" means to you, what would you say?

To me, "Getting Right" is a really important statement to yourself if you're on a journey of self-improvement. It means "getting right" with your attitude, your people skills, communication, and your day-to-day responsibilities.

Please understand this: "Getting Right" isn't about living some make-believe, perfect little life, with no ups and downs, detours, roadblocks, or setbacks. Those are just part of the journey that helps to make and mold you.

When living a life of crime, "Getting Right" can also mean doing a crime and doing it "correctly." This is the power of a negative attitude directing negative outcomes.

The worst case is having a negative leader, leading negative-thinking people to do negative things which they may think is the right thing.

The power of needing to be accepted is so powerful and self-destructive. I know, because first I was led, and then became the leader of negative actions. I was led toward a negative outcome by the power of wanting to be accepted, and became the "get-away driver" in multiple robberies. I was led by my own choices for reasons that don't even make sense to me today, other than my youthful desire to be a part of something and to be accepted.

I believe many people get all caught up in a mess, in jail, six feet under, and/or hurting others—just to be accepted. This is called "peer pressure," and can and has brought down millions of people, young kids, teens, you name it. Peer pressure has a mind of its own, a power that can't be touched or seen, like fear and faith. Peer pressure can be deadly, and it can be pleasing, depending on what you choose to accept—negative or positive peer pressure.

Are you allowing peer pressure to direct your life? Have you done so in the past? Are you led by the desire to please others just to be accepted? I have, and let me tell you it sucked afterwards. The ride might feel good at the time, but afterwards, you're down for the count.

These days, peer pressure can also mean "bullying" which drives people—mostly teens and young adults to do things they otherwise never would have done. Some even commit suicide rather than face the negativity of bullying.

Peer pressure and bullying are negative forms of trying to feel important and powerful. But at the end of the day, everyone loses.

On the other hand, there is such a thing as "Positive Peer Pressure," which means being a positive role model, doing the right things at the right time. It means saying no when it's time to say no, helping others see the right thing to do, and then "getting right" about the right things to do in life.

The "right thing" can be defined in many ways, but let's just say when we know it's the right thing, it doesn't hurt others and it moves us in the right direction. No crimes are committed—it's just simply the right thing to do.

I believe we all know the difference between right and wrong. We have all been blessed with the power to determine right from wrong and make the decisions to take either path. We have the power of choice.

No one can really make us do anything. Sure, they can put pressure on us, hold a gun to our heads, literally and figuratively. They can push us over the edge with words and actions. However, from what I've seen and done, the bottom line is we have to get ourselves out of that environment, and quickly.

Others who think negatively and live negative, self-destructive lives don't just appear and control my life. I first have to put myself in that position or environment before anyone can "control me," so to speak.

Here's what I have to say: "Get right," right? Don't put yourself in a self-destructive environment in the first place. If you find yourself there, then make some new choices. Get the hell out before you truly become a victim of your own choices, which can lead you to a place you really don't want to be!

We all know that we can be our own best friend or our own worst enemy! When we find ourselves stuck in a rut, not believing we can rise any higher, we need to ask ourselves, "Why do I think this way?" "Who programmed me to think this way?" like "I'll never be anything, do anything greater." "I'm just average." "I don't have any talents." You get the picture.

Whenever that happens, we've got to tell ourselves, "I don't have to believe or be programmed by other messages. I can 'get right,' 'get out' and 'stay out' of this funky thinking stage."

Our attitude moves us forward or downward. We've got to change our thinking to change our life, right?

Getting right with our attitude about ourselves, what we want to achieve, where we want to go, and what difference we want to make in life, takes time. None of it happens overnight. Very few people say, "I've worked all my life to be an overnight success!"

Life is tough and tough choices have to be made. If we want to live a good life, make good decisions, and change and grow through our experiences, we need to look forward.

No matter where you are right now in life, good or bad, high or low, locked up or free, the process of getting right and staying right by making right decisions, is just part of the journey.

Remember, when I say "locked up," it doesn't just mean in a physical jail or prison. We can be locked up in many ways—by our "stinkin' thinking." Our relationships, our financial situation, our emotions, or even locked up in our own homes, afraid of the big, bad, ugly world that awaits us.

Just because you aren't in prison doesn't mean you're "free." Being free is living the life you want, being happy, finding your purpose and passion in the world, working in your perfect career, or having a family. Whatever it is that defines free, happy, and successful to you.

How many people do you know who are truly happy? Most folks aren't living a "free" life. They think they aren't successful in the world's eye. Maybe they're lonely or lost without any direction.

Getting right isn't an easy thing to do. Sometimes it takes years and sometimes it takes hitting the wall, screwing up to go up. Many times, it takes "letting go" of the stuff or people that are holding you back (Re-read Chapter 4).

I've got to believe that everyone desires a good life, even the hardened criminal, the one who hasn't gotten caught yet, the one who's hit the bottom and doesn't know how to climb out.

I truly believe everyone wants to make good choices, live a good life, and make the right decisions that can make a difference in their lives, as well as in the lives of others.

Folks, let me tell you, I've screwed up more times than once. Heck, more times than three or four, can't count the times I hit walls greater than the Wall of China!

Nevertheless, I found the will to keep pushing forward. I kept moving along until I found what I thought was my purpose in life, a life of meaning and significance.

I've gone through many ups and downs, U-turns, accidents, bad and good decisions, and positive and negative life experiences to even begin to get on my path of significance. I know I've hurt many people over the years with my screwed-up thinking and actions. I've lost everything, been basically homeless, jobless, pride-less, courage-less, just about any "less" you can think up.

It took many long, hard years of self-destruction before I could see any light at the end of the tunnel. And even then, that light seemed to shine through a tiny peep hole.

But the one thing I know and know deep inside—I never gave up on me. I just didn't know it then, but I know now. Patience is a virtue and my negative actions taught me about patience, hope, motivation, and self-determination.

Following are three key areas I believe are critical to getting right from head to toe:

1) Getting right on our choices
2) Getting right mentally
3) Getting right spiritually

1) Getting Right on Our Choices

What happens on the inside when you lose everything on the outside? Either change and growth, or self-destruction. I chose change and growth!

Thirty days in "The Hole," in solitary confinement, and thirty days of "grue." Grue is a Southern prison specialty. It is served cold to prisoners twice a day. It's made out of cornmeal, maybe some miscellaneous meat, potatoes, eggs, syrup, some vegetables, other leftover stuff, and then baked. One day a week, we would be given a regular meal from the chow hall.

The Hole and grue taught me about hope, and patience. They taught me about putting self-worth before net worth. Those two creepy old friends—the Hole and grue—taught me about getting right and letting go!

We all have a story. We all have that something or someone who made us look up, wake up, and get right. Those two experiences—The Hole and grue—gave me my wake-up call. We all can be an inspiration to someone, an encourager through our experiences and life stories.

We all have the power to make the right decisions at the right time about the right path to take. No one is to blame for our going down the wrong path—not our parents, spouses, kids, the judge, our friends, the establishment, or our environment.

Sure, it's always easy to play the blame game. We can get really good at it, if we choose. We've seen it in action, been in the middle of it, done it, lived it, and some of us have even mastered it!

Let me share this fact of life with you. The blame game doesn't work. There are no winners, no victories, no thinking "I missed the bullet," "It wasn't my fault," or "If it wasn't for them …", "If only…"

Take that thinking out to the outhouse and drop it down the hole. Or dig a hole and bury that story, that blame. Let it go and get right about the right choices that you and only you can make about your life.

If you want freedom, happiness, and success, whatever those mean to you, the first step is in taking responsibility for your actions, whether the outcome is good or bad. It is what it is. ***The choices you make, make you.*** Please remember that statement in your everyday decisions. I did tell you **Your Life Matters**, right?

I read once that we make an average of (over) 2,500 decisions every day. Many decisions are made unconsciously, without even thinking about them! Many of our decisions are based on habits. Guess what? Bad habits are meant to be broken, shaken up, and changed into good or better habits.

2) Getting Right Mentally

You likely have a computer, a PC, an iPad, or even a smartphone. These computers have mechanical brains—not as multifaceted as yours or mine—but nevertheless, a powerful brain. Our minds are like computers. Just like programming a computer, the way we program our minds is the way it's going to function. Garbage In, Garbage Out, *or* Good In, Good Out.

The software or programs we load into our computers determines what comes out. Many of us at some time or another have had to deal with computer viruses. Well, it's the same with our minds. We get what I'll call "Thinking Viruses." How we think about ourselves and our environment can control our minds' computers, our actions, our attitudes, and our behavior.

What we load on our minds' computers directs our actions, our behavior, and our attitude. We have a choice: deactivate that negative software and remove it, then "reboot" our systems. We've got to load in the right software and remove the negative viruses. We can choose to hit the delete button and redirect our lives now!

Trash in, trash out. It's as simple as that! Take out the trash and let in the sunshine!

Here's what I know. We can all live the life we choose if we make the right decisions, surround ourselves with the right people, develop the right skills, and have a positive attitude and patience with ourselves.

Life isn't really all that hard—unless we make it hard. We can do "Hard Time" or not, in or out of prison. Hard time can be found in the free world, as easily as within the gray walls of a prison cell.

We always have choices. Hard time or good times; hard time or loving times; hard time or fulfilling times; hard time or faithful times; hard time or easy times; hard time or fruitful times... these are all choices based on our attitude and environment.

You get to choose your path, your faith, and your courage to say no. Let go and get right with your thinking!

It is a blessing, a gift from above, that allows us to make the decisions we choose to make, good or bad. Some people call this "free will."

3) Getting Right Spiritually

Now I think I need to take you where you may or may not be ready to go—your spiritual side, not the dark side!

Let's talk about getting right with your spiritual side, your faith side. Back in the mid-1970s, it was me, the chaplain, and a horse trough. Sounds like a joke, doesn't it? A preacher, a teacher, and a judge walked into a bar...

Who would ever think a horse trough would change my thinking and then begin the process of changing my life? Not me! But my new spiritual life began that day. I really didn't know it then. But the seed was planted.

Just like anything, once the seed is planted it can take years to reach a tree's full height, potential, or purpose. An acorn can grow into a massive oak tree. Just that little seed. Amazing, right?

I know you're wondering, "What's up with the horse trough?" Friends, the trough was what was used at the prison farm for the chaplain to baptize those who were looking for a new start. Those, who were ready to make a commitment to Christ and to their salvation.

The horse trough was filled with water and was big enough and deep enough to use for baptisms. So it was me, the chaplain, and the horse trough that began my new spiritual life.

It has taken more than 40 years for this to all make sense to me. That's a long time wandering around the planet lost and confused about my purpose, passion, and direction.

My friend, this is what I learned. It took many, many years, but I finally got it. He must have seen something worth saving when He saved me. I was pardoned of my sins. I was free because I finally realized *my life matters*.

Back when I was a troubled teen, lost in life, searching for something better than what I had, imprisoned literally and figuratively, I thought this faith thing must be the way. Somewhere along my journey from nowhere to somewhere, I had to "get right" with my spiritual side, the side of me I knew nothing about.

It was scary and yet in my mind, it seemed like the right thing to do at the time. If I knew then what I know now, I would have jumped headfirst, all in and devoted my life to Christ, to God and myself a long time ago.

Looking back, I liken my life to that of Moses, out in the desert for 40 years, roaming and searching for the Promised Land.

Of course, there are places where it is hard to share and follow your faith openly—like on the streets, in prison, in relationships, in your job. There are places you aren't able to share your spiritual side for fear of confrontation, being laughed at, or being told you're crazy or stupid and that there is no God. Being faithful is a tough road to travel and cross to bear. Remember, it's okay to take the path you believe is right for you, no matter what anyone says or thinks.

Suddenly, I realized this very powerful message: "He was there all along."

If you really want to get out and stay out of whatever situation you're in, a key is to admit you need help. You can't do it all alone. Today, I know God is around me everywhere I go—in me, under me, above me, in others who walk past me, in the trees, wind, the smells in the air, and all creation.

It took me many years to understand this. I hope it won't take you 40 years of roaming in the wilderness to accept that God is the way out and the way to stay out of whatever mess you've got yourself into.

Get right and get God!

About ten years ago, I started writing another book entitled *Do Your Best and Let God Do the Rest*. That's the message I'm sharing with you now. Just do your best and let God do the rest if you choose to develop your spiritual side of life.

Many times, our "ego" gets in the way of our desire to change, our abilities and potential and most of all, our relationship with our Creator. One of my mentors, Dr. Wayne Dyer, taught me that "ego" means "Edging God Out." Today, I understand that more than ever before, so I do my best to keep "ego" out. I say to ego, "Get out, stay out!"

Ego can do a few things to you. Your ego can push others away, keep you from reaching your potential, keep you from loving and being loved, keep you from growing up, and could keep you from your Creator, the one who loves you more than the world itself, the one who made the greatest sacrifice, the one who offers you eternal life.

Why would you trade all this for a screwed-up ego?

To all my fellow life travelers who cross my path and come into my life, I pray and hope that you will get right with God, yourself, your thinking, your dreams, and your love for life.

Get out and stay out of the life you don't want and start living your best life—beginning right now!

Don't edge God out. Open your heart, your mind, and the doors that hold you back. Accepting God can be the best thing to help you escape your self-made prison. Discover true freedom in just being and living a good life.

Begin now to live an intentional life, a life of significance, purpose, and meaning. It can be done. Just look at me! I'm rich in life, living a good life, loving someone, being loved, and writing to you. Just maybe my story and message will set you free to live your best life, the life you really want. Get Right.

Getting out and staying out of a life you don't want means becoming intentional about your whole life and everything that happens within it. *Your life matters!*

Three Simple Steps:

1. The first step is thinking right and having a positive focus.

2. The second step is not allowing anything or anyone to sway you, slow you down, or change your positive thinking!

3. The third step is knowing that it's okay to get right about what you desire in life, your happiness, and the desire to be and have more. The more you can be and have, the more you can give and serve others.

Getting up, getting right, getting out, and staying out is alright!

6. Knowing You Can Do It

With the right attitude, anything is possible.

I've read that by the age of seventeen, the average teen in the United States has been told over 150,000 times; "You can't...," "You won't...," "No...," "Stop...," It's not you...," "You're not ready...," "You won't make it..." The list goes on and on.

These negative, self-limiting phrases can and will stunt the positive growth, self-image, and motivation of many a person.

I believe I was a victim of these circumstances. I'm not using the blame game, because I did know right from wrong. I could see where my attitude was taking me. I also understand that such phrases were not usually spoken intentionally by my parents or other people of authority, like teachers, coaches, and others.

Many times, we just do and say what we were taught. We don't really take into consideration what our words might be doing to another person.

On the flip side, I've also read that the word "Yes" is heard on average 5,000 times. The word "Yes" is a very powerful permission to hear, to say to yourself and others. "Yes" is always better than "no"!

I've got to believe that many of us love the stories we see on TV and online. You know, when one person in a race who's running behind, then the runner starts picking up speed, and those on the sidelines cheer the runner on with encouraging shouts of "You can do it!" "Keep going!"

I believe that everyone wants to cheer on the one who may be struggling, encouraging others to not give up. It's so inspirational.

With tears in our eyes, we want to stand on our chairs and yell right along, "You can do it!" "Don't give up!" It's inspiring to the one you're cheering on, but more importantly, it's inspiring to us, the cheerleaders. When we encourage another person, maybe even a total stranger, it builds us up.

During my cancer battle, I had many people cheering me on, giving me encouragement, pouring positive words into me. "You can do it! You can beat it!" And I did.

We all need encouragement. I read once, "How do you know someone needs encouragement? Answer: If they are breathing, they need it!"

We all have our personal battles where we need encouragement and positive words and actions. And we can all be one another's cheerleaders.

I truly believe most people want to cheer others on, say things that will help them to get moving and win their race. It's just like when you're the one that is being cheered on and inspired to not give up.

When my best friend and life partner Debbie got cancer in 2012, I had to step up my cheerleading skills. It was my time to be encouraging, supportive, and help her fight her own battle. We had to have faith in one another and we had to know we could do it!

I love this quote by John C. Maxwell: "People never outperform their self-image." I share a lot of his quotes, because for me, they're right on! They hold a lot of truth.

It's in our DNA to care for others, cheer others on, help others, inspire others. Look at the way people came together to help one another in the aftermath and devastation left by Hurricane Harvey in Texas, Hurricane Maria in Florida, Puerto Rico, and the Caribbean, Hurricane Florence in the Carolinas, and even after the horrible shooting in Las Vegas.

We need to receive that same fuel, that same encouragement. It's almost like we can empty our "Motivation Bank" by giving. Then when others give back and pour encouragement and support into our lives, we fill that bank back up again!

Everyone needs someone and someone needs you, right now, as you are reading these pages.

We all know someone who may be in a rut, stuck in a bad relationship, in a job not going anywhere, financial debt, drug or drinking problem, or fighting cancer or another illness.

Maybe that someone is you; it's certainly been me as well.

We all have a duty to our family and friends to seek out times to wipe away the tears, times to be a listening, caring, and intentional friend and encourager, times to remind them they can do it. They can get out and stay out. They can stop and turn their lives around. We can assure them that there is hope.

We all need hope in our lives. We need hope, love, and faith. No one fights alone!

I can share story after story in my life, when I needed to hear, "Larry, you can do it!" "Larry, you can change!" and "Larry, it'll get better!"

Who do you know right now who really needs encouragement, just a friend with two caring, loving, and open-to-listen ears?

In our book on what cancer has taught Debbie and me, *It's Not About You, It's About Those You Love*, we emphasize practicing "Sincere appreciation for others." When people are hurting, down in life, behind bars, locked in their bottle, or lost in drugs or an abusive relationship, they don't need anyone telling them what they "should do" or "ought to do."

What they really need is sincere appreciation for themselves, for what's going on, and someone to first listen, then ask, "What can I do for you?" unconditionally. You just might be the one who needs sincere appreciation or a friend. You might be the someone to truly help others and find ways for them to get out and stay out of whatever is hurting them, holding them down, or ruining their life.

Is it you who is stuck, deep in trouble, or lost in life? We've all been lost or stuck at some time. It doesn't matter how rich or wealthy you are, money can't fix everything, and most of the time, what has to change is internal. We need to change our thinking, our sense of self-worth, bring hope and faith in ourselves, and the courage to move forward.

When I was released from prison, I really had no clue what to do with my life. I really had no direction, or anyone to really point me in the right direction.

Sure, I was told I needed a job, but what could I do? I remember my grandpa trying to help me get a job; he took me around to a couple of places, and used his contacts to get me a job. But guess what I did? Once on the job, I figured out who the screw-ups were and hooked up with them. Before I knew it, I was out looking for a job again.

Yes, I had been set free from prison, I was in the "free world," but looking back now, was I really ready? I know that sounds really screwed up, but sometimes when we get out of the crap we're in, we're not really sure if we're ready to get out. I wasn't.

I didn't know it then, though. I just knew I was out, set free into the "free world." I was off and running to nowhere, but most likely heading back to where I came from.

Getting out of anything without a plan can put us right back to where we just got out of!

Ever been there?

Well, I have, and have seen many others get one foot out the door and without having support or a truly realistic plan to stay out, the other foot is right back to where they just came from!

Getting out and staying out of whatever you know isn't right for you isn't a destiny, it's a journey, a process that continues on.

When I talked to my crack pipe about letting her go, it was just talk until action took place. I finally took action after I had lost just about everything I had. Most importantly, I had lost my pride, my self-respect. I had let crack take me down.

Talk is cheap. It takes action and others to help us get out and stay out. Plus we have to truly believe we can do it.

You have to believe it, others can believe in you, but at the end of the day, it's you and you. Back then, it was me and the pipe. A few times the pipe won. Sad, hey?

It was no different when debt was my friend. Bankruptcy became my other friend. What a mess it all was. What a hole I had gotten myself into. All the mess was no one's fault but mine—not the pipe, not another person, and not the economy. No, it was just me and debt.

Do you know debt? Debt is really not a good friend. I finally realized I could let that bad friend go and move on to new friends. Everybody needs a good friend.

Do you know my friend called "bad, screwed-up relationship"? Oh, boy, was that a rough ride! Sure, I could blame the bad relationship on her, but what a rut that became. I made many bad decisions in that relationship. What it taught me was at the end of the day, I needed to have a conversation with the person in the mirror about what was going wrong. Let me tell you, that was a tough conversation. Every time I've had a talk with that person, it was hard, because I couldn't lie, couldn't hide, because I was looking at me, face to face.

That person in the mirror, me, finally said, "You can do it, Larry. You can get out and stay out and shut that door. Quit trying to justify who's at fault and get out and get moving." And that's just what I did. You can, too.

Can you name a few "friends" you really didn't or don't like? Bad friends like I just shared with you—my crack pipe, debt, bankruptcy, and a bad relationship.

You have my permission. You can do it. Go ahead and say yes and start naming those very bad friends of yours. It's okay. It's the first step to acknowledging your problem. Then begins the process of letting go and growing from it and getting out and staying out—*because your life matters*.

Life is all about stepping in mud puddles, falling into ruts, driving through potholes, failing forward, and learning through experience. When stuck, you only have two choices: stay stuck, or make the decision to get unstuck! Pick yourself up and get moving.

You can do it! You can do just about anything and then again almost everything.

Life is full of surprises. Can you remember being a kid and being excited on Christmas morning? You were up before sunrise and your parents, eager to see what surprises with your name on them were under the tree.

That's my favorite time of year. I can remember the fun and surprises, not just for me, but also for my sister and brother. Surprises are wonderful and the much greater surprise is to discover the power that lies within you. I'm talking about the power of your faith, your abilities, and your potential. You have the power to make the changes that will make your future. You have the power to pull the weeds and make room for personal and spiritual growth.

You can do it! You can change your thinking and change your life, I'm walking proof. Someone you know is walking proof of change—someone at your workplace, in your neighborhood, church, community and all around you. Change is just a choice. It can be scary as hell at times, but still a choice!

Through change comes growth, personal development, and the opportunity to be more, give more, and live more—*because your life matters!*

You have the power to be more than you are today, to live your dream life, to learn to lift others to reach for their dreams. Just as you may need encouragement in your life today, someday you'll be the inspiration and the encouragement to another in need. Everybody needs somebody sometimes!

Just like that surprise Christmas present under the tree, other surprises await you today. Those presents are all around you, and opportunities that pass us by every day. Some we call lucky breaks, others we call fate or the universe working its magic. Some of us say God is in control of our every step when we allow Him to be.

Allow me to share another "God lesson" with you. God doesn't take us along a straight line. There will be twists, turns, disappointments, losses, and bad breaks. They're all a part of His plan for us.

Life is one big surprise. The thought that you can do it, you can change, you can make a U-turn, redirect your thinking. Yes, you can have faith, you can believe, and you can let go of what or whoever is holding you back. You can do it!

Trust me. I can tell you story after story of how change is possible.

You can change, you can grow, you can take the path you choose to follow. You can paint the picture of your future exciting life. You can develop the environment you choose to live in, and you can help others along their journey, too.

You can reach for the stars. Heck, you can be a star. You can build your dream home, you can be the dad, brother, boss, friend, spouse you really want to be. You can program your mind to give you the returns in life you plan for. You can even ask for help and guidance from God. You can pray about your life, your purpose, and ask for direction and understanding. If you don't like this part, that's okay. I'm not trying to push my faith on you; I'm just saying it worked and is working for me.

I can share many stories of the amazing gifts God has shared with me. Yes, me. Someone who committed some pretty bad stuff and took actions that drove me to break many of the Commandments in the Bible. But He was there when I needed Him the most. God never deserted me. He states, "I'll never leave you." Finding God has been key in my personal development and faith in myself. Faith power works wonders!

Following are pieces of the puzzle that helped me, and I believe, can help you as well. Here we go!

1) On Permission

Another concept I've found that has been very important to me and my personal growth is *permission.* You may be thinking, "What kind of permission?"

What I'm talking about here is this: I found the permission to be me, to hold my head high, and the permission to realize that it's okay to be okay.

Many people have crossed my path and many have offered me permission. When others showed they believed I had potential, that was permission. When my mother told me to hold my head high at a very difficult and trying time in my younger years, that was permission.

There are so many times and people in our lives that offer us permission to be more. We may miss it, or we're not ready to hear it yet, or maybe, we just don't understand what positive permission is.

We can't do anything great alone. We need others and we need people to give us permission and encouragement. We also need their love, just as they need ours in return. This is how we can get things done in life.

Most important is that we learn to give ourselves permission to grow, change, create a better life, and take the opportunity to be more. At the end of the day, self-permission comes first. This is the permission we give ourselves to be who we really want to be.

I believe we can do just about anything we really want to, as long as we have a few things in our corner. The following are what I believe are the keys to unlocking the door to our potential:

1. Faith and belief in ourselves

2. The courage to take action

3. The confidence to follow through

4. The right skills

5. A positive attitude

6. Other people who believe in us and are in our corner.

7. Self-motivation

2) On Intentions

Good intentions are just good thoughts. Actions and an intentional attitude to move forward are key to your happiness and success.

If you're in a bad relationship, what do you do? Do you make the case that its's best for the kids to stay together, it's easier to just wait for it to get better, or face the fearful

question of what can you do? If the relationship is beyond repair, then it's time to let it
go. If the relationship is abusive and you stay,
then you're just hurting yourself more. I give
you permission to let go. Give yourself
permission to get out and stay out! You can
do it! Good intentions to get out won't move
you out—you've got to take action. One small
step at a time.

What if you have a bad addiction and you
don't know what to do? You first remind
yourself you can do it, you can let it go. I
found with my drug addiction, to let go I had
to replace it with something different, something good and positive for me. I've found the
best way to beat a bad thing in my life was to
replace it with a good thing.

Let me give you an example. My thinking
was negative. I had no self-worth. I learned to
replace that "stinking thinking" with positive
and healthy thinking by reading and listening
to positive messages. I began to enjoy reading
uplifting and positive material and slowly but

surely, developed a new and better self-worth.

Maybe right now you're in a bad place at work, maybe you aren't having fun anymore, or you're not growing within the company. Maybe you feel like a victim, the boss is against you or something. Start looking for something new. Get busy planning your life, not just getting by in life. I give you permission to do so. You can do it!

You've got skills, you are valuable and have something to bring to the table. Make the move that will help you be happier, more satisfied, and passionate about what you do most of your waking hours. I give you permission to do so. You can do it!

Get intentional about what you want and take the steps to get there. Remember, good intentions are great thoughts, but intentional action moves you forward!

Everyone has value. Everyone is valuable. You can also get better. You can grow and develop your skills and value, so that you can go find the job, or the position that will allow you to showcase your value. You can do it!

Don't settle with just good intentions— become intentional in your thinking, actions and behavior. You will see a change in the right direction!

Learn to live an intentional and thought-ful life. Give yourself permission to take action and your good intentions will turn into great rewards!

3) On Competition

Jay Leno says, "Competitive people will overcome any odds." To get out and be our best and stay out, we must learn to be com-petitive. We must learn to be competitive with ourselves. To always be our best, running our own race, no one else's. We don't have to follow the expectations of others, just simply run our own race.

Maybe right now, you smoke and you know it's not good for you, but you just can't seem to shake the habit. I smoked for many years—hardcore Camel non-filters. Actually, I almost got high on those strong cigarettes! You combine the Camels and pot and I was a smoking machine.

When I was ready to let the smoking go, I knew I had to replace that habit with something good for me. I turned to walking and biking. When the urge to smoke came, I walked. When the feeling for that after-dinner cig came a-knocking, it was time for me to walk and think good stuff, breathe fresh air. You can do it, too!

Once I quit, I never went back. That's part of the process of letting something go. You can't move forward if you're always making the choice to go back to your "old friends" and bad habits.

It really doesn't matter what it is you're stuck in. The same process of decision-making that got you where you don't want to be, can be the same process of making new choices

Your Life Matters

and decisions to get you out and keep you out. I give you permission. Give yourself permission, too. You can do it!

Don't compete with others—compete with yourself! Seek to improve yourself every day.

4) On Self-Talk

What you say to yourself matters more than anything anyone else can say about you or to you. Your words can lift you or destroy your dreams. Your words can move you or stop you in your tracks. The things you think turn into the words you say about your life position, your situation, and your abilities to get out or stay stuck!

I don't remember where I got the following statement, but I find it very powerful. It's now just passing through my mind and heart to yours. Hold it!

If you fill your mind with the right thoughts, there won't be any room for the wrong ones.

Powerful, right!? Now let's look at Proverbs 13:3:

> *He who guards his mouth*
> *preserves his life,*
> *but he who opens wide his lips*
> *shall have destruction.*

Our thoughts and words can and will move us in the direction of our thinking and what we're saying about where we're going. It's important to feed our faith, feed positive reinforcement of our situation, and feed our courage with powerful, positive words of self-encouragement. You can do it!

Hit the delete button when words or thoughts arise that don't serve you anymore. Delete the messages that say, "I can't" or "I won't." Hit the delete button when those negative words pop into your head. Instead, choose the words and thoughts that are good for you, the new you, the new normal. Choose those words and thoughts that will lift you and move you forward into your desired, happy, and fulfilling life.

Yes, you can do it!

Three Simple Steps:

1. First step, allow your self-talk. Tell yourself you can do it, you can become the person you truly want to be. Be intentional about your actions.

2. Second step, don't accept any negativity anymore. Remove it from your life. Don't hang with folks who will move you towards a life or position you don't want to be in anymore! Run your own race.

3. Third step, tell yourself every day, "I can do it!" Give yourself permission to let go. Believe you can march forward; you can be the person you see yourself being.

You can do it! Yes, you can move into the life you really want to live.

7. What Would I Be Saying Today?

We each have the power to change. It's simply a choice.

S o, what would I be saying today to that young teen that might help him find his way?

The first thing I would say is, *"You'll be okay!"*

Another thing I might say: *"It's going to be alright. You'll find your way!"*

That young teen would be me. What would I be saying today to that struggling, lost soul?

Oh, yes, I would have loved to be able to sit down with that young, lost soul, with all that I have learned since those days. But we all know that can't happen. Surely there is someone else I can mentor and share my life experiences with to help along life's journey.

Of course, there were many who came up beside me and shared words of wisdom and encouragement. I'm guessing now, looking back, I didn't listen to them too well.

Not always do younger folks listen to older folks, teachers, coaches, or their parents. I know I was guilty of that! Sometimes we have just got to learn the hard way. We learn through life's experiences, and from good as well as bad choices and decisions. But you know that, right? If I could have, I would have slapped me upside the head a few times and said, *"Listen, boy. You're really screwing your life up. You've got to stop."*

I'm not really sure that would have helped, but looking back now, it may have knocked some sense into me. Hopefully, time will tell the story.

There are many times I just want to say to someone, *"Come sit with me, let's talk. How are you doing?"* I have a deep passion to reach out and help lead others to move in better directions or just live a better life.

Do you have kids, or someone in your life that you can see is moving in the wrong direction? Maybe it's smoking, drinking or drugs. Or maybe it's spending more than they make, or fighting with their spouse or kids. Everyone has a story, a battle, something going on in their life. Everyone knows someone that needs help or encouragement to get on the right track, or just a better track.

Oh, yes, if I were sitting with me about 43 years ago or so, I would be saying:

- *"I know it looks like you're all alone, but you're not."*
- *"You've got a friend you haven't met yet who is with you daily."*

No one fights alone. I would hug this young guy, and do my best to make sure he felt loved and deserving, valuable and needed. I would be sure to let him know, *"You're going to get through this mess and find your way, and your life is going to be different and better and you'll make a difference one day!"*

I believe everyone has a purpose. And I also believe that everyone has skills and gifts that they can become really good at. We all have a life that matters, no matter what direction we've chosen to follow, how deep in a rut we can find ourselves in.

I would tell that young teen today, *"You've got some really good stuff inside you just waiting to burst out!"* and *"One day, you're really going to make a difference in your life and those who cross your path."*

And you know what? Anyone can. I did, and I have no regrets of my past mistakes and experiences, and you shouldn't either. No matter what your past looked like or was, it doesn't direct your future. Your thoughts, attitude, passion and determination will help you live the life you truly want to live!

I know for sure now that my past doesn't define my future, or my potential. It is what it is. But there are many great lessons I have learned that helped me be the person I am today. Same with you. It doesn't matter what you did, how much trouble you got into—yesterday is done and over with. The key is realizing what you did learn, what you can share to help lift another out of what may be the same rut you got yourself into.

The best life we can live is sharing and helping others through life, seeing the opportunities to make a difference on purpose, and being intentional about living a life of giving. I know that young teen 43 years ago would have looked at me and said: *"Sure, whatever, you probably had an easy life. You had people in your corner, or money, a good life, and what do you know about me and my life?"*

And he would have had that right. So many times, people come to us and say, they know how we feel—and the fact is, *they don't*. I couldn't have known for sure. I just know that when you're down as low as you can go, and you have no more self-esteem or motivation in you, you feel like you suck, and life sucks. Most of what people may say doesn't mean much. What has to happen is we've got to find our way, find our *why*, our purpose, our strengths, our blessings, and it may take years. For some they may never discover their potential. That's why it takes people like you —learners and givers—to come along side others and help them along, wipe away the tears, listen, mentor and just be a friend.

Yes, we can make a difference and that young, lost teen today is on a mission to make a difference on purpose. I'm living an intentional life of personal growth. I'm looking and listening for the opportunities to give, help and add value through my life experiences. Thus, the purpose of this book, *Your Life Matters*, is that you too can get out of the life you don't want and live the life you do want. I hope my life story can help lift you out of a rut, and help you find your way and truly live the life you want.

What would I say today? *Let Go, Get Right, Believe in Yourself, Faith Matters and You*

Can Do It. Yes, **Your Life Matters**, so get out there and make a difference, starting right now!

Wait! Hold up before you start your new race, your new journey. It might not be a bad idea to go back through the book and reread some of the points of interest you highlighted or where you dog-eared the page.

One last thing: begin thinking of who you know who could use this book and its message in their life. Note their name in the front of the book so you don't forget to make an investment in others by getting them their own personal copy.

Now together, we are adding value to others you know. We are making a positive deposit in their life. You are helping them move beyond the rut they are in and helping them climb their personal Mt. Everest. The bigger their mountain, the greater the challenge and the growth that can come out of it. Help them along. Now you get moving and living the life you truly want.

It's okay! You can do it!

Three Simple Steps:

1. Speak magical words to yourself and others.

2. Inspire yourself to be just a little more each day. Reach out to others at every opportunity and make a difference.

3. Decide today that you'll be okay and find your way! Your life matters!

The choices we make —
make us!

8. Transformation is Real!

Transformation is an intentional act of self-love.

How do I know transformation is real? Hello, my name is Larry and I'm living proof that transformation is possible, logical, achievable, and real!

Transformation begins within. In 2013, I was a member of the John C. Maxwell Team that went to Guatemala to teach more than 20,000 people. We were on a leadership journey to help that country begin a transformational process to move forward in its desired direction.

Because of that journey and time in Guatemala, I know that what happens on the inside is more important than what happens on the outside. Also, what happens on the inside begins to show on the outside in our behavior, habits, communication, and leadership of our own lives.

Before we can be transformed, we have to be willing to let go of our not-so-good thinking and any faulty attitudes about ourselves, our habits, behavior, and even addictions. I believe we must allow God to help us disrupt our lives, shake us up, set us free, and get right.

I believe this book is all about transformation—the transformational journey we take by getting out of the life we don't want, staying out, and living the life we do want.

Transformation is up for grabs for anyone who truly has the desire, motivation, and will power to change their lives for the better. We all find ourselves in some rut at some point. We also find ourselves feeling lost in our purpose at times. Transformation is about change and growth. Change happens, but growth is optional!

We all know change is going to happen—that doesn't mean transformation is going to happen, though. I believe true transformation comes from the desire to grow through our change.

Wherever you're at in life today doesn't define you or mean you have to stay there. Even if you're inside your own self-made prison, transformation and growth await you. You can change, grow, and transform into the true person you really want and desire to be. Hope awaits all of us. In hope and faith, I believe you can change and grow into the person you really want to be. That is transformation!

Transformation is real and it awaits you, me and everyone. We can transform our thinking, our attitude, and our life position.

You can make transformation happen in your life right now. It all starts within. With faith in yourself, your ability to believe in yourself, courage, confidence, trust, and the willingness to get out of the life you don't want and start living the life you do.

There are **two key factors** to help you in your transformational journey: People and Skills.

1. People

You need others (people) to help you along your journey. You need encouragers, cheerleaders, and connectors who can help connect you to the right people who can help you find the right help, job, or even a new friend. You need others you trust to believe in you, talk faith in you, speak words of wisdom in your life. You need your cheerleaders, your change-fighting teams, to lift you and help you along!

Everyone needs someone. Somebody needs you, you need someone, and it's what connects us all together.

Transformation isn't done alone. You've got to have others in your corner, and the key is finding the right ones. They may not be family, or current friends. You may need to step out of your comfort zone to find new people who will help you get where you want to go or who you want to be. They are those who have achieved what you wish to achieve.

Now think about people you would like to help you along your transformational journey. Maybe they are people you know, or someone you know who knows someone you'd like to meet. Perhaps the person is an author, speaker, coach, or mentor you would like to connect with. Take a few minutes to write down their names below, then be intentional with an action plan to make it happen.

1) _____
2) _____
3) _____
4) _____
5) _____
6) _____
7) _____
8) _____
9) _____
10) _____

2. Skills

You need to evaluate your skills—those things you are really good at—and develop a plan to get even better! You can achieve just about anything if you have the will power, the skills, and others to help you.

Your skill factor is key. Your skills are what help you become valuable in the market, to land the right job or career so you can have the funds to live the life you desire. Look around—there is a book, a coach, and most likely a video on how to do or improve just about anything.

If your skill is in communicating, there are books, videos, online training courses, and people like me who can help you grow in your skill. No matter your skill, you can improve on it, grow into it. This is transformation.

Let's stop here and get intentional. Take some time to write out your high-value skills, along with a few words about what you think you can do to increase your value in those areas. This is just good, old goal-setting to identify what, how, and when. You can do this!

My skill	How can I improve?	When will I do this?

Your transformational journey has already begun. It began when you made the choice for change, the decision to get out of the life you don't want and to live the life you do want. It began when you picked up this book and began reading and thinking, "I can do it! I can become more. I can leave the life I don't want and live the life I do want!"

My transformational journey began later in my life, around 1987. I didn't even know it was happening because no one had ever spoken about transformation to me. Now I can look back and see it was happening. When I joined the John C. Maxwell Team, I learned more about transformational leadership and how it starts and what it is, does and can do for me, you, and others.

You can begin your transformation right now. It's your time. Better late than never, right?

You might be thinking, *"So, Larry, what is this transformation you're talking about?"* Let me share my definition with you.

Transformation is Real!

Transformation is going from me, to you, through you, and to others. It's about living an intentional life of significance, not an ego-driven life. It's about changing and growing so that you can be more, give more, add more value to others, and hopefully leave some type of legacy.

Once I've gone to my home in the sky, my heavenly home, my desire is to leave a part of me, my legacy! That's one of the reasons for this book as well.

After many years, I stepped out of the life I didn't want, I got out, stayed out, and I'm beginning to live the life I want. I'm living a life of value towards others, a life that brings me true happiness and meaning.

It didn't happen overnight. I spent more than 40 years roaming the planet, lost and confused with no real purpose and understanding of what my life could mean to me and others. I'm in my baby steps on my transformational life journey of just wanting to make a difference on purpose intentionally every day of my life.

I don't know what you want. Maybe you don't yet either. But I've got to believe if you're living an unhappy, abusive life, a life of confusion, if you're lost, broken, homeless, in prison, or even your self-made prison, you want something better for yourself. I hope I'm right. Am I?

If this is so, I hope my story will give you encouragement, hope, faith and the permission to get out, stay out, and go live the life you want. Now! Don't wait to start. Make this an urgent change and decision.

If you're still struggling on how to start, reach out to me. I offer coaching and am confident that I can help you plant the seeds to be able to move in the direction you'd like.

We don't know when our time is up. Therefore, we must make the best of each day we are blessed with, in hope of being more, giving more, and making a difference in the world—or maybe just in one person's life.

Transformation is real. Trust me, you can do it. You've just got to start. Take the first step to get out and stay out of the life you don't want and live the life you want!

I believe in you. I know if I can do it, you can do it. I know if you believe in yourself, you'll be amazed at your potential. I believe if you'll have faith in yourself and God, you'll see faith power work wonders in your life today and every day!

Are you ready?

Begin your transformational journey of change and personal growth so that you can truly live the life you want. Change your thinking and you can change your life starting today!

> *Be ye transformed by the*
> *renewing of your mind.*
> —Romans 12:2

Three Simple Steps:

1. The first step is being true to yourself, accepting yourself and your future exciting potential.

2. The second step is knowing what you have. Your experiences, wisdom, and life are meant to go through you to share with others and make a difference.

3. The third step is knowing you *can* make a difference. You can change and transform your life into being a person of value who values others.

Transformation begins within, moving from me to you— and through you to others!

Recommended Reading

There was a time in my life that I did not read. Today, I love reading—fiction, non-fiction—anything. Every book offers something. Maybe it's excitement, sorrow, learning, mystery, spiritual—it's all good. Below are just a few books that have helped me with my personal development and growth over the years. It's exciting to see how my personal library keeps growing!

- The Bible
- *How to Win Friends and Influence People* by Dale Carnegie
- *From Good to Great* by Jim Collins
- *Inspiration* by Dr. Wayne Dyer
- *Big Magic* by Elizabeth Gilbert
- *The Journey* by Rev. Billy Graham

- *I'm OK, You're OK* by Thomas Harris

- *Born to Win* by Muriel James and Dorothy Jongeward

- *The 15 Invaluable Laws of Growth* by John C. Maxwell

- *The Strength You Need* by Robert J. Morgan

- *The Laws of Lifetime Growth* by Dan Sullivan and Catherine Nomura

- *The Purpose-Driven Life* by Rev. Rick Warren

Acknowledgments

This book, the stories within, and the seven chapters would not have been created without the people in my life who have helped me become who I am today. There are so many who have played a role in my getting out and staying out of the life I was living and live the life I really want.

I first thank God, who accepted me as I am, forgave me, and lifted me up from the bottom of the pit.

Second, I thank Joanne, my mother, who has been in my corner at every turn, always loving me, believing in me, and trusting in me.

My sister Rene, who always seemed to show up when I needed someone the most in my early years, and even to this day, is a true friend.

My best friend, life partner, and cancer-fighting partner Debbie, who has put up with the roller coaster ride we've been on now for over 24 years. Debbie is also the co-author of our second book, *It's Not About You, It's About Those You Love*, on what cancer has taught us about life.

A few others I can't leave out: Bill, a lifelong friend, who trusted me and believed in my potential before I did. Peggy, who taught me how to love the one you're with and helped me believe I could be more than I was. My friend, Gary Wilder, who allowed me to become the professional I was meant to be by giving me a chance.

My book publishing team, Kira Henschel, owner of HenschelHaus Publishing, our friend, publisher, and editor. Andrew Welyczko, owner of Abandonedwest Creative, is the creative side who helps us with cover and interior design.

Acknowledgments

"Nothing great has ever been achieved alone," says John C. Maxwell, my mentor, who shared with me that "Just start writing" is the first step to birthing a book.

About the Author

Larry Cockerel is a self-proclaimed change agent. He is the author of three other books, and works with people and organizations to leverage change. He teaches people to accept change, work with change, and make change an asset to improve their businesses, communication, results, and creating an exciting picture for the future!

Leadership and sales development are two other areas in which Larry has a true passion in helping people and organizations develop, disrupt, grow and change for the better.

Larry is a Certified John C. Maxwell Team Leadership Coach, Speaker, and Trainer, and a Cancer Survivor Inspirational Speaker, sharing that change is okay. Larry believes that attitude is everything when it comes to change and moving the obstacles out of the way to be the best you can be.

Larry and Debbie reside in Cedarburg, Wisconsin, and work together to encourage change and help others by making a difference on purpose and intentionally. They are both cancer-fighters and speak at American Cancer Society Relay for Life Events in Wisconsin. They share the many lessons cancer has taught them about enjoying their gift of life and how facing and overcoming cancer can help others.

* * * * *

Invite Larry to present at your next event. Please feel free to contact Larry with any questions, booking for keynotes, training and development by visiting

www.larrycockerel.com
Tel: +1 414-531-7859
Twitter @larrycockerel
Facebook: Larry S. Cockerel

You can also email questions or comments directly to Debbie@larrycockerel.com.

We would enjoy the opportunity to speak to your group, coach, or offer training development for your organization. Just reach out any time—let's work together to add value and motivation at your next event. *We can do it!*

*9 7 8 1 5 9 5 9 8 6 7 2 6 *